AF664326

Writers of Indian Diaspora: Theory and Practice

Writers of Indian Diaspora

Theory and Practice

Edited by

Jasbir Jain

RAWAT PUBLICATIONS
Jaipur • New Delhi • Bangalore • Guwahati • Kolkata

ISBN 978-81-7033-454-5

© Contributors, 1998

Reprinted, 2017

No part of this book may be reproduced or transmitted in any form or by any means, electronic or mechanical, including photocopying, recording or by any information storage and retrieval system, without permission in writing from the author(s).

Published by
Prem Rawat for **Rawat Publications**
Satyam Apts., Sector 3, Jawahar Nagar, Jaipur - 302 004 (India)
Phone: 0141 265 1748 / 7006 Fax: 0141 265 1748
E-mail : info@rawatbooks.com
Website: rawatbooks.com

New Delhi Office
4858/24, Ansari Road, Daryaganj, New Delhi 110 002
Phone: 011-23263290

Also at *Bangalore, Guwahati* and *Kolkata*

Typeset by Rawat Computers, Jaipur
Printed at Nice Printing Press, New Delhi

To the bonds of sisterhood

This is for my sisters who - whether at home or abroad -
have always been with me

Contents

Acknowledgments

The idea of this book originated in a seminar on "Expatriate Writing: Theory and Practice" in December 1996 at the University of Rajasthan. Several of the essays included here were initially presented as papers in the seminar which was jointly supported by the University Grants Commission and the Indian Association for Canadian Studies. The Shastri Indo-Canadian Institute supported the seminar with a gift of much needed books. Their help is gratefully acknowledged here.

Others who have supported this project are—Mr. Kailash Rawat of Rawat Publications who is supporting a series of works on Writers of the Indian Diaspora for which this volume provides a useful background as it discusses theoretical perspectives; my colleagues and friends who have not only contributed to the volume, but many of them participated in the seminar, generating a great deal of interest and enthusiasm among the younger scholars and raising issues of great theoretical significance.; Dr Chandra Mohan, the President of the Indian Association for Canadian Studies, and who in his personal capacity was extremely supportive of the whole project. My thanks are due to all of them as also to those friends who though unable to come for the seminar, have contributed to the volume.

Introduction

Expatriate writing occupies a significant position between cultures and countries. It generates theory and defines positions as it constructs a new identity which negotiates boundaries and confines and relates to different temporal and spatial metaphors. Cultures travel, take root or get dislocated and individuals internalize nostalgia or experience amnesia. Writers living abroad live on the margins of two societies and cultural theory is today being created by people who live on the margins. An important question is how does one define the margins. Do the margins expand themselves and does the centre shift? Or is it that peripheral areas further divide themselves and the centre remains the same, indifferent to what is happening around it? Does theory emanate from the intervention of marginal voices, or is it that their voices are controlled and homogenized by the centre? These and a host of other questions crop up when we focus on diasporic writing.

Increasingly the terms which are gaining popularity are 'expatriate' and 'diaspora'. The word 'diaspora' is literally a scattering carrying within it the ambiguous status of being both an ambassador and a refugee. The requirements of the two roles are different. While one requires the projection of one's culture and the ability to enhance its understanding, the other seeks refuge and protection and relates more positively to the host culture. Further categories emerge through the use of such words as immigrant, exile, refugee. Their use attempts to give some indication of the ideologies, choices, reasons and compulsions which may have governed the act of migration. While 'immigrant' defines a location, a physical movement and a forward-looking attitude, 'exile' indicates a compulsory isolation and a nostalgic anchoring in the past. The word 'exile' evokes multiple meanings which cover a variety of relationships with the mother-country—alienation, forced exile, self-imposed exile, political exile and so on. In the Indian context perhaps all meanings are true with the migratory movements having been governed by different reasons at different times of history, and different reasons even contemporaneously. Economic reasons governed the movement of indentured labour and of the trading communities; they have also governed the pursuit of a higher standard of living. Opportunities for work, research and freedom have motivated migration. Again migration from a colonial state to a free country calls for an entirely different set of assumptions than migration from one free country to another.

The diasporic community is varied and complex and hence all attempts at homogenization are likely to lead to over- simplifications. Bhiku Parekh has observed that the Indian diaspora is one of the most varied, representing "half a dozen religions... seven different regions of India... nearly a dozen castes" (Parekh 105). It has shown a great mobility and adjustability as it has often been involved in a double act of migration--from India to West Indies and from there to metropolitan centres; from India to Africa and then to Europe or America on account of social and political reasons. Parekh also comments upon their networking with each other, their sense of solidarity which reverses the concept of homelessness. The diasporic Indian is "like the banyan tree, the traditional symbol of the Indian way of life, he spreads out his roots in several soils, drawing nourishment from one when the rest dry up. Far from being homeless, he has several homes, and that is the only way he has increasingly come to feel at home in the world" (106).

Yet this multiplicity of 'homes' does not bridge the gap between 'home'--the culture of origin; and 'world'--the culture of adoption. The boundaries have an uncanny habit of persisting in thousand different ways, and are very often conflictual. Homi Bhabha shifts this conflict to a theoretical gain, he transforms the diasporic scattering to a gathering, "Gatherings of exiles and emigres and refugees, gathering on the edge of 'foreign' cultures, gathering at the frontiers; gathering in the ghettoes or cafes of city centres" (139-140), and thus he shifts the focus from nationhood to culture, from historicity to temporality, a hybridity which cannot be contained either in hierarchical or binary structures. Others like Rushdie turn to India, to a mythologising of history. Naipaul transforms his sensibility to a perpetual homelessness while Bissoondath rejecting the homogenization of ethnicity, projects immigration as "essentially about renewal", about change. It is unjust, he points out to expect that the communities from which the immigrants emerge be required to stand still in time, to do so is "to legitimize marginalization; it is to turn ethnic communities into museums of exoticism" (Bissoondath 111). Ashis Gupta in an interview turns the discussion to the insider/outsider syndrome and points out that acceptability or rejection by a host culture depends upon the 'value' of the person, his use to the new society, his educational level and his social milieu.

Abdul Jan Mohammed describes the expatriate's position as being one of either the "specular border intellectual" or the "syncretic border intellectual". The latter is more at home in both cultures and reaches out to both simultaneously, combining and synthesising them while the specular border intellectual. "finds himself or herself unable or unwilling to be 'at home' in these societies." Such intellectuals are engaged in defining other possibilities (JanMohamed 97), and in their position (and functioning) as exiles they are likely to be critical of the new culture. Citing the example of Edward Said, Jan Mohamed comments,

"Quite often his position, which allows a kind of distance from Western literature and discursive practices, permits Said a specular role—that is, he is able to provide in his writing a set of mirrors allowing Western cultures to see their own structures and functions" (105).

Thus immigrants and expatriates define their positions variously but there is something more to it. The important questions which are often relegated to the background are how is the home country affected by diasporic space and does it, in anyway, assist the process of decentring? The Special Fiction Issue of *The New Yorker* (June 23 & 30, 1997) is a clear indication of the manner in which the stay-at-home writers are affected (one would soon have to coin a term for them like NEI, [Non Expatriate Indian] or RI [Resident Indian] as opposed to NRI [Non Resident Indian]). Of the dozen or so writers represented, Salman Rusdhie, Amit Chaudhuri, G.V. Desani, Kiran Desai, Amitav Ghosh, Vikram Chandra, Jhabvala, A.K. Ramanujan all live or lived abroad. To balance this there is a solitary article on (and not by) R.K. Narayan, and a couple of poems. Bill Buford in his editorial asks the question "What does it mean to be an Indian—to be citizen of a country that for thousands of years was no country, that has not one language but at least eighteen, and that no single race or religion or culture but many races, many religions, many cultures" (*The New Yorker* 7-8). Rushdie's "Introduction" to the Viking edition is reproduced here and is titled "Damme, this is the Oriental scene for you!" G.V. Desani's piece represented here is "India, for the plain hell of it". The special Granta issue on India is somewhat more representative. Focused on India it has several contributions by foreign correspondents and journalists, other contributors are Nirad Chaudhuri, Ved Mehta, Amit Chaudhuri, Suketu Mehta and the twice-removed V.S. Naipaul. Of the writers in India are R. K. Narayan, the writer-publisher Urvashi Butalia and the Britisher Mark Tully. The Viking anthology concentrating on creative writing spans a longer period but is both unsatisfying and incomplete. Works like these provide ample evidence of the fact that diasporic space is pressing on the space of the home country. It is not that the centre has shifted, only the margins have expanded to push the home cultures further to outer space. The West continues to be the place for exhibition, recognition and judgement.

There is need to realise the significance of the cultural encounter which takes place in diasporic writing, the bicultural pulls and the creation of a new culture which finally emerges. It is equally important to understand the dynamics of reception at both the ends for reception is also rooted in cultural contexts. This double discourse of reception needs to interact not only to throw light on the meaning of this writing, but also to throw light on the non-diasporic writing and the formation of cultural theories. Diasporic writing exists and it cannot be wished away. Given the fact of its existence and its occupation of the intervening space, it is perhaps necessary to create another centre, another subjectivity. Reviewing and critiquing diasporic writing is part of this process, for it should relate and reflect and not transform and absorb.

Postcolonialism which is often referred to as the "theory" of migrancy, does not necessarily equip one with adequate means of approaching and interpreting diasporic writing for two very important reasons (i) writing generates its own parameters for aesthetic evaluation as the act of writing itself is a negotiation with cultural constructs; (ii) postcolonialism is variously defined through political and historical conditions as well as aesthetics, and its legitimacy needs in itself to be questioned. The whole question of postcolonial aesthetics needs to be subjected to a careful scrutiny. Critics have located its beginnings in Fanon's *The Wretched of the Earth* (1961), its theorizing in Edward Said's *Orientalism* (1978), critical assessment in Ashroft, Griffiths and Tiffins' *The Empire Writes Back* (1989). Critics have occupied contradictory positions, and rightly so for contradictions beset its application. Meenakshi Mukherjee located in India views it as an "emancipatory concept" while Arun Mukherjee situated in Canada resents its monolithical structure (see Trivedi and Mukherjee 1996, Meenakshi Mukherjee 3 and Arun Mukherjee 13-20). In Arif Dirlik's view postcolonialism is the child of postmodernism and it marks the arrival of the third world intellectuals in First World academe (329). The transition is viewed from 'colony' to 'Third World' to 'postcolonial' societies. In all such perceptions the margins are underscored, the affiliations with postmodernist aesthetics bypassed, and the world situation perceived through fragmented approaches rather than locate the beginnings,of both postmodernism and postcolonialism in the post-World War II political situation. The point of origin is not power, but the collapse of Empires, not the West but Asia and Africa.

Diasporic writing has developed its own theoretical position privileging a double vision. But these theoretical explorations work in different ways and throw up questions which affect both personal and social concerns and have political and cultural implications. The expatriate as he moves from one culture to another may need to locate himself/herself afresh in relation to the centre. Gurbhagat Singh looks at the different ways Edward Said and Homi Bhabha approach this question. While Said's position takes note of the schizophrenic nature of the expatriate's reality and the "crossing over" from one culture to another which way be a liberating experience, Bhabha is more concerned with the instability which at some point defines the expatriate self. It is the disunitive hybrid moment which is important to Singh, and which upsets the conventional relationship between the centre and the periphery.

The two creative writers, Uma Parameswaran and Ashis Gupta, both located in Canada, work from their own experiences. Parameswaran provides a much-needed gender perspective to the whole discourse. Women have the ability to relate to two homes simultaneously. She also brings out the static quality which nostalgia confers upon a culture and the manner in which self-imposed ghettoization interrupts the process of acceptance of and by the host culture. The experiences of migrancy vary from person to person, depending upon the levels of education, age, background and point of entry. But neither dislocation nor absorption can be total; there has to be an ongoing involvement with reality. Ashis Gupta, on the other hand, begins with a nostalgic reviewing of the past, and contextualizing his responses in his personal experiences he looks at the relationship of the expatriate to his home country. One never leaves one's country behind; yet one cannot live in the past. Gupta resents the West's continued impulse to interpret India through its stereotypical fixations, an impulse which slants diasporic vision negatively. It is this which needs to be resisted, both at the personal and the creative level. For Gupta, the fractured self is a reality. Later on in the volume in a candid interview with Veena Singh, he examines the outsider/insider syndrome wherein he emphasizes the 'value' of the individual, in terms of usefulness, and elaborates how it facilitates acceptance on both sides.

Taking up a comparative framework, P.A. Abraham places the work of Mavis Gallant side by side with that of Bharati Mukherjee. Physical dislocation is not the only dislocation, and the level of affluence not the only determinant. The loneliness of Mavis Gallant's characters is shared by Mukherjee but acceptance or rejection are often located in social forces. Migration from one developed country to another may raise a different set of questions than the migration from an underdeveloped country to a developed one. For one, the economic advantages are no longer a significant factor.

The dynamics of language are placed in a very interesting framework by David Stouck who relates expatriate writing to the theory of receptivity. It is no longer how we see ourselves but how others do so, and in this transaction language, which is a cultural construct, is a significant medium. The cultural nuances are often imperceptible to the foreign reader, yet the expatriate writer, very often deliberately disrupts his narrative to include words and expressions from his native language consciously creating a barrier for the foreign reader and requiring the reader to make an effort to understand. This strategy succeeds in large measure in defining generic boundaries. Genres are also often culture specific, some forms flourish better in certain cultures, the 'romance' as novel as the tale of an individual, has flourished in the West, while the novel as epic, as community dominant, has flourished in the East.

B.R. Nagpal's essay as the South Asian Women poets, Rajul Bhargava's on Bharati Mukherjee and Rohinton Mistry, Shyam Asnani's on three expatriate writers and Jasbir Jain's on Ondaatje and Gupta are all placed within comparative frameworks. Each one of them explores different aspects of expatriate writing. While for Nagpal the sense of alienation is transformed into mixed images representative of two cultures and bridging the differences between them, Bhargava through narrative structures looks at the assimilatory and disintegratory stances adopted by Mukherjee and Mistry respectively. Shyam Asnani's consideration of Kamala Markandaya's *The Nowhere Man*, Bharati Mukherjee's *Wife* and M.G. Vassanji's *No New Land* interprets them as individual encounters and relates them to the narrative structures. For Jain the location of Ondaatje's *The English Patient* and Gupta's *Toymaker* in the seemingly "neutral" Europe, is a conscious strategy out of the schizophrenic split, but which unconsciously reflects the expatriate's concern with the colonial/victim syndrome.

Anisur Rahman while focusing on Ondaatje's *Running in the Family* highlights the autobiographical involvement and the adult dissection of the past, so necessary to the creation of the expatriate self. Sudha Rai employs a modernist approach to *The English Patient*, highlights its intertextuality and exposes the underlying contradictions.

The past exists, and it also persists in different modes and manners. Gupta's *Dying Traditions* located in India but reaching out to Bangla Desh and America and to the pre-partition India, in Veena Singh's analysis, works simultaneously at several levels - historical, personal, cyclical. Violence and terrorism live side by side with mysticism and renunciation. For Uma Parameswaran the past is metamorphosized through a process of remythologising. Jancy James works through the images projected in *Sita* and *Meera*.

Rohinton Mistry is the subject of Ameena Kazi Ansari's essay as well as Savita Goel's piece on *A Fine Balance*. While Ansari's concern is with the narrative structures and subjects, Goel examines Mistry's detailed and intricate reconstruction of the India during the emergency reflecting its multiculturalism and humanistic substances.

Chandrika's interpretation of Vassanji's *The Book of Secrets* both as a journey into the hero's past and the writer's past engages itself with the structural and linguistic strategies which centrestage the diary as hero, the real book of secrets. Sonal Baxi's essay on Neil Bissoondath which connects his fictional work with his non-fictional *Selling Illusions: The Cult of Multiculturalism*, and which disaffiliating security and insecurity from material well-being, affiliates it with political factors, and Jameela Begum's interpretation of Selvadurai's *funny boy* complete the volume.

Selvadurai and Ondaatje both are from Sri Lanka, Vassanji an Indian who moved to Canada through Africa, Neil Bissoondath an East Indian from West Indies. The rest — Rohinton Mistry, Uma Parameswaram, Ashis Gupta, Bharati Mukherjee, Kamala Markandaya and the women poets are all from India.

Most of the papers included here were first presented at a seminar held in December, 1996. Some like Uma Parameswaran's piece, Jameela Begum's and Ameena Ansari's essays were later contributions. Together they present the expatriate's fractured and decentred self, and the expatriate vision with the intensity of nostalgia and the play of memory.

Jasbir Jain

References

Bhabha Homi. *The Location of Culture.* London: Routledge, 1994.

Bissoondath, Neil. "The Uses of Ethnicity", *Selling Illusions: The Cult of Multiculturalism in Canada.* Toronto: Penguin 1994.

Buford, Bill. "Editorial, *The New Yorker: Special Fiction Issue*, June 23-30.

Dirlik, Arif. "The Postcolonial Aura: Third World Criticism in the Age of Global Capitalism", *Critical Inquiry.* Vol. 20. 1-2, Winter 1994.

Jan Mohammed, Abdul R. "Worldiness - without - World, Homelessness-as-Home: Towards a Definition of the Specular Border Intellectual", *Edward Said: A Critical Reader.* Oxford: Blackwell. 1992

Mukherjee, Arun Prabha. "Postcolonialism: Some Uneasy Conjunctures" in *Interrogating Postcolonialism: Theory, Text and Context* ed. Harish Trivedi and Meenakshi Mukherjee, 1996.

Mukherjee, Meenakshi. "Interrogating Post-colonialism", *Interrogating Post-colonialism: Theory, Text and Context.* ed. Harish Trivedi and Meenakshi Mukherjee, 1996.

Parekh, Bhikhu. "Some Reflections on the Indian Diaspora", *Journal of Contemporary Thought*, Baroda 1993.

Trivedi, Harish and Mukherjee, Meenakshi. Eds. *Interrogating Post-colonialism: Theory, Text and Context.* Shimla: Indian Institute of Advanced Studies, 1996.

1

Expatriate Writing and the Problematic of Centre: Edward Said and Homi Bhabha

Gurbhagat Singh

Expatriate writing, in its theory and practice, is the work of the exile who has experienced unsettlement at the existential, political and metaphysical levels. With this experience, he/she has unsettled the philosophical and aesthetic systems. The phenomenon of exile has emerged in our times due to uneven development within capitalism, and due to the movement forced by colonial powers. The uneven development has led to unprecedented migration of the Asians and Africans to the West. The imposed, and indirectly hegemonizing shift from territories, has occurred within Asia, Africa and the Middle East, and also from these continents to the West. This movement has produced a new person whose mind works at least with two epistemologies. He/she has lost the centre that used to unify. Contingencies of history have affected to the extent of dismantling the comforting and stable perspectives. The dismantling has led to some unknown and intermingled visions. The hybridity experienced is not just philosophical, it is also local and existential. At a very fast pace, literary aesthetics has leaped toward an abyss in which the Parmenidian and Apollonian sort of poetic principles that are non-contingent and logical but shaped by the Enlightenment, have ceased to matter. Theory is being re-cast with a non-theoretic or unfoundational stance to keep the contingent and existential under focus.

The migrant existentiality that is determining this specific aesthetics without making itself a lasting essence is faced with two centres: the external colonial or modernist, and the internal or national filtering into a personal identity. The chief feature of the poetics of exile is the trial during which it deals with these centres, sometimes rejecting and sometimes accepting them.

Edward Said's writings are a very interesting example of this trial. As a Palestinian, born in Jerusalem and self-exiled to the U.S.A., he has always aligned himself with the Palestinian movement for liberation and a sovereign state. The experience of movement that is partly self-chosen and partly imposed on him by history has become very "important" to him. His way of looking at culture and creativity has been altered. In an interview with Salman Rushdie (Said 1995:122) he says: "The whole notion of crossing over or moving from one identity to another, is extremely important to me, being as I am – as we all are, a sort of hybrid." The significant expression here is "as we all are" in which he generalizes hybridity, the intermixing that he believes shapes all of us. From his personal-existential situation he universalizes. But what appears to fascinate him in this "crossing over" is a demonadizing or de-essentializing. The discourse of the disunitive subject recently initiated by Lacan and extended to the "differantial" linguistic (dis)unit not accomplishing the "will" or "desire" implying both Nietzschean and Freudian notions, shapes the "hybrid" of Said. The "crossing over" and contaminated para-subject of exile that he theorizes is in resistance to the colonial centre that marginalizes. It prevents "counternarratives" from emerging, says Said. Elaborating the relationship of the imposing centre and its affective narratives he comments on the American context: "The executive presence is central in American culture today, the president, the television, commentators, the corporate official, celebrity. Centrality is identity, what is powerful, important and *ours*... And centrality gives rise to semi-official narratives that authorize and provoke certain sequences of cause and effect, which at the same time prevent counternarratives from emerging" (Said 1994:393).

Said's "counternarratives" are those of repressed cultures that are either subsumed by the meta-centre or threatened to subsuming. In this statement Said appears to be arguing with the notions of Lyotard elaborated in his *The Postmodern Condition* and a later essay "Universal History and Cultural Differences", although there is also a point of difference. Whereas Said looks at the hegemonizing centre from the standpoint of a political exile, and Lyotard from the angle of an "amnesic" located in the modernist pathology. Centre, to Said, generates a strong sense of "identity" on the part of those in power. By quoting Adorno from his Minima Moralia, Said points out the manipulative and totalizing danger of this "identitarian" politics. His exile subverts this "logic of identity" and represents what he calls, using Immanuel Wallerstein's phrase, "anti-systemic forces" (Said 1995: 153).

The colonial, imperial, totalizing or homogenizing centre is what Said's exile aims at dismantling. But the exile's problematic is how? Through constructing the small identity that is native or national which has been contaminated or eaten up, or through a lasting disunitive consciousness? About this Said takes two positions. In conversation with Rushdie on the Palestinian Identity (1986) Said emphatically stated: "Whether in the Arab world or elsewhere, twentieth century mass society has destroyed identity in so powerful a way that it is worth a great deal to keep the specificity alive" (Said 1995: 122). Only a year earlier than this conversation, Said had talked about the dangers of "difference" around identity even if it was small (1995: 100). What he means is that an exile in his battle against the meta-centre can use his mini but distinctly grounded cultural- historical centre as an armament to liberate. Using small identity to "privilege" oneself or one's community over others is not creative, it is for that reason that this identity is to be refused. In his Reith lectures delivered in 1993, Said devoted one lecture to the theme of "Intellectual Exile", although all the six lectures build up a theory of the intellectual enterprise around the expatriate's experience. In this Lecture III, that is six years after his above conversation with Rushdie, Said emphasizes the exile's "dyspepsia" or in his own words "a kind of curmudgeonly disagreeableness" that makes him "dislike" the trappings of accommodation and national well-being (Said 1994:39).

If Said's exile is constantly disagreeable or "dyspepsic", he also gets "pleasure" in his venture. At the end of his work *Culture and Imperialism* that he published in 1993, he supportingly quotes a 12th century monk from Saxony Hugo of St. Vicar where he elaborates the journey of the exile from his "homeland" to the globe. The exile first becomes "tender", then strong, and finally perfect: "The person who finds his homeland sweet is still a tender beginner, he to whom every soil is as his native one is already strong, but he is perfect to whom the entire world is a foreign place" (Said 1994:407). In the last paragraph of this book Said says: "there seems no reason except fear and prejudice to keep insisting on their separation and distinctiveness as if that was all human life was about. Survival in fact is about the connection between things..." (*Ibid.* 408). Working through attachments is alright but it is more meaningful and evolutionary to interrelate. Said ends up at a Bakhtinian kind of heteroglossal dialogue of different identities in which they connect with each other and become hybrids. If he rejects the meta-identity of the centre, he also belittles the small national identity of a battling community. In his view, the small identity tends to separate and privilege itself and thereby alienates from the inter-community mosaic. Said's exile appears to be moving from hybridity to heteroglossia of the world.

But the problem with Said's exile is that while he/she gets pleasure from this doing, he/she enjoys the experience of "instability" and "surprise", especially the "juxtapositional double perspective" (Said 1994:44).The person does not know how to stay in the unstable world. He/she does not get to an ungrounded multilogue whose differences could be pleasure some in their meaning and aesthetic relationships. For this lacuna and philosophical-poetic inadequacy, Said takes the exile back to a

Universalism or the kind of meta-centre that he had earlier rejected for its hegemonic and manipulative power, probably under the influence of Gramsci and Marx. A Fanonized national specificity that Said had asked for keeping alive, he also abandons. In the "Introduction" to the Reith lectures he says: "The attempt to hold to a universal and single standard as a theme plays an important role in my account of the intellectual.... Universality means taking a risk in order to go beyond the easy certainties provided us by our background, language, nationality which so often shield us from the reality of others. It also means looking for and trying to uphold a single standard for human behaviour when it comes to such matters as foreign or social policy" (Said 1994:xii). Said's exile defines himself/herself in a very dignified schizophrenia in which he/she subverts the manipulative meta-centre but also accepts to legislate a single behaviour. It again minimizes "specificity" that privileges over others and generates identitarian politics, but also accepts it to resist the meta-centre. I have called this schizophrenia "dignified" because it is influenced by the intention to be maximally human and other-oriented. The schizophrenia of this exile is parallel to the schizophrenia of the Capitalism's resistive schizo who is pushed to the borders of rebellion in Deleuze's and Guattari's *Anti-Oedipus*.

The poetics of expatriate elaborates itself without centres in the writings of Homi Bhabha. In his celebrated essay "Dissemination, time, narrative, and the margins of the modern nation" Bhabha defines culture or nation in terms of "double inscription." It means the theoretic-historical constitution related to origin or event that he calls "pedagogical", and the disruptive "scraps", patches and rags of daily life, that are "performative" (Bhabha 1990:297). Bhabha projects culture as hybrid from the side of migrant and subaltern. Even the postcolonial Manichean view of Fanon has been assimilated into his theory. Fanon, in his works *The Wretched of the Earth* and *Black Skin, White Masks*, explains the identities of both the colonial and his victim as hybrid, they have two simultaneous references, because to Fanon the "body" is set up in the world and its contingencies. This Manichean double inscription or two references is to live on borders. Bhabha uses the term "liminality." He elaborates culture, its member, and its sign all in terms of the tension of differences: the differences of historical past and the present, and of the subjecting and the subjected but clashing or meeting in a capital Now. He has used a very significant term for this Manichean meeting: "disjunctive temporality." He says about this temporality: "It creates a signifying time for the inscription of cultural incommensurability where differences cannot be subsumed or totalized because they somehow occupy the same space" (Bhabha 1994:177).

Bhabha's "disjunctive temporality" is analogical to Salman Rushdie's notion of "broken mirror" about the migrant. Rushdie even generalizes the excitement of the "homeless" when he says: "But human beings do not perceive things whole. We are not gods but wounded creatures, cracked lenses, capable of fractured perceptions" (Rushdie 1991:12). The migrant's or expatriate's "cracked" and fractured seeing has been called by Bhabha, using Lacan's notion, as "the twilight existence of the aesthetic image" (Bhabha 1994:15).

Bhabha's major contribution is toward defining the migrant sign and subjectivity. Diaspora, according to him, produces "incompatible systems of signification." By this he means meaning-production through "interstitial" perspectives. Interstitial articulation of the sign is in the movement of signification without concentration on one signified, constant "erasure" in the Derridean sense. It could be the "subaltern instance of metonymy" (*Ibid.* 65) which means fragmenting power- loaded signifieds and contaminating them with the Other, the hegemonered, and then making them fantastic, as is done by Rushdie. Bhabha illustrates his notion of interstitiality of sign and subjectivity by quoting from Toni Morrison's *Beloved* where different characters claim the beloved: "Beloved, she my daughter", "Beloved is my sister", "I am Beloved and she is mine" (*Ibid.* 17). The sign "beloved" here signifies from "the in-between space", its interstitiality. In the process the sign becomes disunited. The "desire" or "will" of the articulating I does not get accomplished.

There is a "time-lag" in this kind of incommensurate and disunitive sign. "Time-lag" is another important term that Bhabha uses to elaborate the specificity of the expatriate semiotics. It is a slowing down of time or teleological linear progress using Benjamin's concept. Bhabha also calls it "blasting" the moment for a new beginning that cannot be made without seizing the present. It is a "caesura" of modernity's unified or forward signification. The hybridity of the impurified sign and its "stillness" is also a moment of "catachrestic seizure" (*Ibid.* 17). *Short Oxford English Dictionary* (1981) explains catachresis as "incorrect use of words." Bifurcating the sign, doubling its signified, tethering its internal organization, are all ungrammatical or incorrect gestures that make the sign "multi- accented" or "Janus faced" in the words of Stuart Hall.

The disunitive hybrid moment sometimes comes very close to mysticism. Bhabha says that it is "outside the sentence." It is "not quite experience, not yet concept, part dream, part an analysis, neither signifier nor signified" (Bhabha 1994:181). Bhabha comes close to this notion of the disrupted expatriate semiotic while elaborating Roland Barthes. He brings out the indeterministic dimension of Barthes to assert that this sign stages epistemological confrontations. Using Roland Barthes' words, he says that the sign is at once "very cultural and very savage" (*Ibid.* 182). Perhaps what he means by hybrid's being "outside the sentence" and its confrontations is a supplementation, some kind of silence that enunciates the jarring and loud, the clashing differences that are "operatic" but co- existent.

By elaborating this interrupted and split sign that is neither signifier neither signified, Bhabha pushes his poetics beyond binarisms or polarities that think in terms of monads. Even Foucault's genealogical power-analysis and its epistemes look to him integral and not circumventing the clashing and co-existing temporalities or the simultaneity of the past and the present, of the ancient and the modern, of the colonial and the counter- colonial.

The stable structures of Marxist class, Althusserian ideology and Lyotardian narratives appear to be situated in centres. Bhabha's culture theory and his poetics based on the postcolonial and postmodern displacements, is completely de-centred. Like Said he does not look back to re-introduction of Centres. He successfully steers his theory out of the Saidial schism. That way his theory cuts its own theoricity and remains unmonolithic. It may be accused of imitating the postmodern and postcolonial homeless. Like him/her it is bare, without a teleology.

Bhabha may also be blamed for robbing the still struggling nations of cultures of their unified identities that they need to battle and self-assert. That blame may well be rightly placed but at the same time, it can also be said that he gives a glimpse of the poetics and cultural theory that are post-struggle or post- apocalypse,where history comes nearly to a close.

References

Bhabha, Homi.*Nations and Narration*. London and New York: Routledge. 1990.

—.*The Location of Culture*. London and New York: Routledge. 1994.

Deleuze, Gilles and Felix Guattari.*Anti Oedipus*: *Capitalism and Schizophrenia* translated by Robert Hurley, Mark Seem, Herbert R. Lane. London: The Athlone Press. 1984.

Fanon, Frantz.*The Wretched of the Earth*, translated by Constance Farrington. Harmondsworth: Penguin. 1962.

—.*Black Skin, White Masks*, translated by Charles Lam Markman. London: Pluto Press. 1993.

Lyotard, Jean-Francois. *The Postmodern Condition: A Report on Knowledge*, translated by Geoff Bennington and Brian Massumi. Manchester: Manchester University Press. 1986.

Rushdie, Salman. *Imaginary Homelands.* London: Granta Books and Penguin India. 1991.

Said, Edward. *Culture and Imperialism*. London: Vintage. 1994.

—. *Representations of the Intellectual.* The 1993 Reith Lectures. London: Vintage. 1994.

—. *The Politics of Dispossession*. London: Vintage. 1995.

2

Home is where your feet are, and may your heart be there too !

Uma Parameswaran

Author's Note: This is a piece that I wrote while on a visit to India in 1995-1996, and that I more recently revised when Professor Jasbir Jain asked me for an essay. It is a meditative piece on the meaning of "home" in the context of the diaspora, how my creative writing sometimes reflects and refracts this theme, and how some areas need to be explored by students and critics of Diaspora Literature. The intersections may not be very clearly spelt out in the following, but then, this is not a critical essay, written as per M.L.A. Style sheet, but a creative contemplation.

Back in my childhood days in Jabalpur, we were force-fed a great many details and data, including the multiplication tables up to sixteen times sixteen; the histories of India, Britain and Europe; the geography not only of India and Europe but of the world, where we were told such trivia as that Winnipeg, in central Canada, was "the wheat granary of the world." Because of the massive infusion of relevant bedrock of mathematical and literary skills, and seemingly irrelevant trivia about the rest of the world, many of us – of the Indian diaspora – have been successful in our careers and have found our individual relevances from our early education. I found, for example, that the wheat granary of the world in the remote Canadian prairies can indeed be "home."

Some of the countless force-feedings consisted of regular doses of poetry to be learned by rote for recitation classes and competitions. Most of these poems have receded into unaccessed depths of my memory, but two have surfaced periodically. One is from Sir Walter Scott:

Breathes there the man, with soul so dead,
Who never to himself hath said,
This is my own, my native land !
Whose heart within him ne'er hath burn'd
As home his footsteps he hath turn'd
From wandering on a foreign strand!

The second poem is "Bingen on the Rhine", by a minor poet, about a soldier of the Legion who lies dying in Algiers, and asks his comrade to carry his farewells to his family and beloved. It says:

The dying soldier faltered and took his comrade's hand,
And said, "I never more shall see my own, my native land."

These lines surface when I hear news of a fellow-Indian dying in north America. "I carry India with me wherever I go", Raja Rao has said. When I got news about my Uncle C's death in Chicago six months ago, I remembered he too had expressed the same sentiments as Raja Rao, and I wondered if he had thought about his native land. But now, writing this piece while in India, I have another question: If, say, I should lie dying in Europe, would I remember the lakes and hills of Jabalpur, and the seaswept sands of Mylapore Beach that was once so clean? Or would I say, "I never more shall see the endless blue skies over my Assiniboine?"

I don't really want to know, not just yet. For there are promises to keep, and miles, I hope, to go before I sleep.

When one arrives in a new land, one has a sense of wonder and adventure at the sight and feel of a landscape so different from what one has been accustomed to; there is also a sense of isolation and fear; and intense nostalgia is a buffer to which many retreat. (The different voices in my *Trishanku* express these different emotions in different ways.)

Some never grow past the phase of nostalgia. Romanticizing one's native land has a place, so long as it does not paralyze one's capacity to develop new bonds within one's adopted homeland. Nostalgia as the only sustenance can become quite toxic, vitiating the living stream into a stagnant cesspool.

Nostalgia, as cesspool, might work in two ways. I have known some who have a propensity to downgrade and denigrate all things north American. I pity them, for they can never be happy anywhere. Even more to be pitied are the ones whose over-romanticization of India throws them for a loop when they have to face the darker side of conditions in their ancestral homeland. V.S. Naipaul's much hated *An Area of Darkness* is an expression of this. While expelling out the toxins from his own system and restoring a measure of health, as his later *India: A Wounded Civilization* shows, he certainly led a great many into yet another misrepresentation of India.

One of the areas that can productively be explored is the gender difference in the kind and degree of nostalgia; as I look back at my own *Trishanku*, I notice that while Chandrika is willing to bond with the land to which her husband, Chander, has brought her, and can love both homelands, Chander cannot commit himself to either. Perhaps women, with centuries of cultural indoctrinations and expectations are able to adapt more quickly and to accept and love two homes without conflict or ambivalence.

Writers tend to focus on the pains of discrimination and alienation, because "our sweetest songs are those that tell of saddest thought." But readers have to keep in mind that each poem is a momentary flare of intense emotion or thought, and that it does not always reflect societal reality or the writer's long- range beliefs. One has to find a pattern that validates that leap into a valid generalization.

Here is where we run into practical difficulties. For Diaspora literature, and I am thinking not only of Indo-Canadian, but of other Asian-hyphenated literatures of north America, anthologies are often the only resources available at this stage of Diaspora consciousness. Anthologies have the imprint of the editor/s on them; and we have to be aware that editors often select texts that are poignant, for the same reason I spoke of earlier, "our sweetest songs are those that tell of saddest thought." There is another aspect that is more inflammatory, and needs closer studies. I call it New Orientalism.

Who is behind the influx of published works that highlight the experience of oppression and victimization of the Diaspora? As in a whodunnit thriller, everyone is a suspect:

Author? One remembers the charges levelled at Indian writers who chose to write in English in earlier decades, and between the lines was the charge that the writers chose viewpoints and plots that would appeal to the English-reading world, wherein lay recognition and remuneration. Do authors, intentionally or unintentionally, assume the voice that readers wish to hear?

Editor? Study the ratio of "immigrant" poems to "poems" in various Diaspora anthologies; have the writers written on other themes? A related question is not as easy to quantify: Are there writers who write about other aspects of life but never get published?

The publishing establishment? The founders? The last two are especially pertinent to the Canadian context, where the publishing establishment depends on subsidies from "arm's length government bodies", where the money comes from the tax payers, but the administration of which is meant to be independent of government agendas. Arnold Itwaru, in *Closed Entrances*, comes to the conclusion that arm's-length funders are not really so. Also, Canadian publishers have to compete with the American market, and sales revenues seldom cover even the production costs, leave alone profit. Canadian culture is kept alive through a quota system to be followed by television stations, the blocking of American super-bookstores that wish to expand into Canada, and book subsidies; the controversy over the issue of keeping Canadian culture alive on life-supporting devices paid for by the taxpayers at large, rather than by the readers and viewers, is an on-going one, and there are no resolutions in sight. But what is clear is that while publishers look for marketability, reviewers and editors tend to highlight the victim or exotic (home is elsewhere) syndromes in work by Diaspora writers. Consider, for example, the reviews of Rienzi Crusz's poetry; his craftsmanship is usually overlooked while his Sun-Man-IceMan metaphors are foregrounded.

Literary texts have tended to focus more on the underside of this gargantuan experience of expatriation, alienation and transplantation. Perhaps the only literary work that has taken a celebratory angle, Bharati Mukherjee's *Jasmine*, goes overboard in the opposite direction, validating the American dream while panning all things Indian. Chitra Divakaruni, the most recent star in the Diaspora sky, delves into the darker dreams and nightmares of womanscape and has an appreciative readership among feminists, but since her women characters are mainly Indo- American, there is a tendency to see them not as individuals so much as representative of the Diaspora, and we are back on square one perpetuation of negative stereotypes that the average north American reader has of Indian life and culture.

From my experience as a university professor, I think that one of the major obstacles I face is of getting students out of a mindscape where other ages, and other cultures, are well- meaningly but dismissively or patronizingly endowed with an aura of "in those days" or "in that culture." And for eighteen to twenty year-olds, even the British culture and the nineteenth century is beyond "here" and "us." The piece I am now working on, for a Women's conference at Leeds, is "Same Space, Another Time/Place." Unless we educate ourselves to see the chronological and geographical continuum, we will see only through a perforated sheet, in fragments. Cne of the novels I am working on is about an early Indian feminist whose story my narrator,

Maru, is trying to tell from her Canadian home.

This aspect of intergenerational communication leads me to another side of our Canadian experience – the chasm between generations.

Within the Diaspora community, the concepts of "home" continue to exacerbate inter-generational frictions that, let us remember, exist everywhere. Inter-generationality has several groupings other than the usual one depending on age. Thus we have disparate "cultures" within the Diaspora.

Children born in Canada are somewhat different from those who come to Canada in childhood; much depends on the parents' economic, educational and cultural background; as also on the time at which they left India.

The place of residence changes configurations; one of my young friends, for example, talked about how life was much simpler when she was growing up in a rural community where her family were the only Indians. She was part of a larger stream, though everything within the house was Indian. Since her family moved to the city, she said, her parents' whole world has become Indian; and not just Indian, but regionally affiliated with the culture of the state from which they had come. It was a constricting ghetto experience that she resented. She is not atypical of her generation. Most young people whose parents keep to the old ways feel trapped by their differences, not only at school but at home. However, with the resilience of youth, most of them find a balance, and some even start appreciating aspects of their heritage culture. If only parents too could be more resilient and flexible to their own and their children's Canadian realities ! What is ironic is that the ghetto existence is self-imposed, as my character, Vithal, says in *Rootless but Green are the Boulevard Trees*.

A new diaspora sub-group that is now emerging in Canada is that of men and women who have spent their working lives in Canada. Except for British Columbia, which has had four generations of Indo-Canadians, in other provinces we are witnessing the first generation of retirees from the Canadian workforce. Thus we have moved into a time when there are of two types of "seniors" as those over middle age are called – those who have spent their working life in Canada, and those who have come to Canada after retiring from India, to join their adult children. The cultural differences between the two could be even more problematic than those between parents and their Canadian-born children, because whereas adults can to a degree shape children's lives and attitudes, reshaping adults' by other adults is a far more contentious issue. While many writers and scholars are focusing on the first pair of generations, not much is available about the second pair of generations, nor of the differences between the two types of seniors.

Having worked with and among the younger generation born or brought up in north America, I am aware of the vast differences between their attitudes to "home" and their parents'. While many have felt the stings of racism in their school environment, most choose the survival technique of downplaying it. Often, this works to their advantage because both oppressor and victim outgrow their roles; but some of the victims carry the scars of trauma all their lives.

Indo-Canadian youth, as I said earlier, often feel the stings of racism (as did many central Europeans and others who did not know English when they first came to Canada.) The desire to act and dress like everyone else is one way for visible minority children to make themselves invisible; and another is to downplay racial slurs as one would skinniness or obesity or various disabilities that are targets of torment.

The children of the first generation of expatriates had the added edge of their parents' work ethic and heredity to do much better academically than most of their classmates. This is true of most immigrant communities, especially from Asia. In the original homeland, education is often the means, the only means to many, of getting out of a cycle of poverty. This work ethic has had its own repercussions on the younger generation, as numerous young people have been discussing in recent years.

Television documentaries (a very popular and prolific part of the Canadian art scene) are now addressing these conflicts. British Columbia, especially, is the centre of much activism and art in this area. A useful source for knowing the British Columbia diaspora art scene is a publication called *Kinesis*, that has a newspaper format and is published ten times a year. The response to video documentaries and stories has been positive – that racial minority children in schools feel a surge of self-confidence when their culture is explained and validated. As one of my former students said when reviewing *The Geography of Voice*, "I wonder what it would have been like had I seen the names of my people on the reading lists, because it would not only be their work that would be recognized as Canadian, but also their names, their heritage, my name, my heritage." (Kalyani Pandya in CV2 16:2, 1993).

We need to bring ourselves into the public arena, to place our works where they can be seen. It is not enough to cry "Wolf" at the moon, as we all too often do in the racism issue. Minority issues need cooperation from within. To give a few examples, *Kinesis* is a nationally distributed forceful periodical that deals with a great many minority issues, and has a great many dedicated workers. *Montreal Serai* is a small publication that protests political inequities. *Toronto South Asian Review* now renamed *Toronto Review of Contemporary Writing Abroad*, is a finely formatted quarterly. There are other, more sporadic, publications that come and go. But the paid-subscribers' lists of these publications are disproportionally small for the amount of work and content each puts forward.

Are the general members of the Diaspora doing anything to help activists and writers? Regrettably, the answer is in the negative. While most events involving song and dance activity, and all events related to religious activity, get volunteers and donations, the Diaspora generally does not lift a finger to help writers and activists (terrorist or cult activities excluded.) In our present context of literature, books and journals by members of the Diaspora are seldom bought by fellow members, and most community papers are distributed free, supported by advertisements. While advertisers get their returns from free newspapers, because of the large circulation, they also perforce have to support every publication produced by religiously affiliated organizations even if the circulation is low because they need to show their goodwill. I know; I have just finished editing a community publication, that has thirty pages of motherhood-is-sacred articles and reports, ten pages of unpaid for greetings from politicians, eleven pages of paid-for greetings from community members, and twenty four pages of advertisements from businesses.

My point is that the cost of production equals the printing costs of a volume of poetry or fiction, and the profits from the advertisements can pay the annual subscription dues of thirty periodicals. But writers and activists seldom get breaks. It seems regrettable in a country like Canada, where the Diaspora has the material affluence to project a stronger presence in the public arena. We have good poets and writers of fiction, children's books etc. but the ethno-centric community is not supportive of the literary efforts of their members. Individuals and businesses that are willing to pay several times a year to have their names in front of fellow South Asian Canadians' readers of community newsletters are unwilling to provide even a tenth of the amount to buy a book or support a writer. They need to recognize that home is where our feet are, even if some hearts just might be half way around the world.

Thus, supported by neither the ethno-centric community nor the larger community, literary efforts of the Diaspora are stifled at birth while the publishers, of course, prefer the marketability of negative stereotypes.

Perhaps these dark realities will change in the future, with the rise of the younger generation born of the 1970s immigration boom. "Home", for those born in Canada, is very definitely Canada, but because of force feeding by their parents, "homeland" could still be India. Further, it does not help that they are often asked, "Where are you from?" as though the colour of their skin automatically pushes them to another place. They are sandwiched between two rocks, but with youth's resilience, I believe they will seize the day. The leaders are out there somewhere, for I have heard their voices on the internet, the new literary medium. Articulate, intelligent, passionate, they seem to me far richer than most of the books of fiction or sociology published on the Diaspora. In these internet postings, I see a validation of what I intuitively wrote about in *Trishanku* and *Rootless*: some, like Jayant, have a love-hate relationship with India, while others, like Vithal, assert and demand their inheritance. Margaret Atwood's Susanna Moodie says of her dead son, "I planted him in this country/like a flag." Vithal is one such flag. Personally, among my characters, all of whom I love (except Chaman Lal), I have a special soft corner for Vithal, whose passion, occasionally violent though it is, knows that home is where the feet are, and we had better place our heart where the feet are:

> I shall bring Ganga,
> as Bhagiratha did of old,
> to our land
> our Assiniboine,
> And the fluteplayer
> Dark as kaya blossom
> Shall dance on the waters of La Salle.

3

The Extraordinary Composition of the Expatriate Writer

Ashis Gupta

A month or so ago, I received in the mail a beautiful photographic book on India - "India: A Celebration of Independence, 1947-1997." It had been published by Aperture Foundation of New York, and the book contained exquisite photographs by the likes of Raghu Rai, Sunil Janah, and Cartier- Bresson. What made it more precious for me was that my young daughter, Shona, had worked tirelessly as the project coordinator without whom the book or the accompanying exhibition of photographs would not have become reality. I was filled with pride, and a great sense of satisfaction at what our daughter had contributed to the dissemination of Indian images and, perhaps, Indian culture.

I soon realized, however, that this sense of satisfaction was purely vicarious. I was trying to expiate a nagging sense of guilt, but knew in my heart that I didn't really deserve forgiveness. This is the guilt of the expatriate Indian, the cornerstone of the immigrant personality. Of course, I realize that I should not speak for others. I know just as many Indians who share my sense of guilt and nostalgia as I know others who present a public persona which appears perfectly content and at ease in Western society. I suspect that all of us somehow paper over the 'cornerstone' of guilt, but that some of us, like me, end up doing a lousy job.

It was perhaps something of a coincidence that, even before the arrival of the gift from my daughter, I had grown increasingly pensive over the fifty odd years of my life. This mood of dark introspection hangs over me every August, no doubt because I was born in that month. But on this year, 1997, much of the world around me seemed full of nostalgia and enthusiasm about India's independence in 1947, fifty years ago. I was surprised how little joy I could summon into my thoughts.

It occurred to me that the word 'independence' was like a needle probing the inner recesses of my brain and taunting me to confront certain facts. One fact was particularly troubling– the way I had rationalized to others that I had really left my country in a quest for independence. By 1971, the year I left for Boston, I had grown tired of standing in long lines myself to buy rationed rice, wheat and sugar. I had grown equally weary of sending out my young servant to stand in line for rations or do other chores that was part of living. I think there was a sense of irremediable social injustice that I had begun to find intolerable. The critical fact must have been the subliminal predisposition to the West that my twelve years of the finest Jesuit education had made me susceptible to. From 1961 (following my father's death) to 1971, I had led the comfortable life of a 'boxwallah' in New Zealand, Australia and India, and could therefore leverage my savings to transport myself to graduate studies in the United States. What's more, I could not bear to endure the Kafkaesque world of my insurance company another day.

Today, I live in Canada, having left my home in Calcutta, not fifty, but a little more than twenty five years ago. I honestly do not know if I am any more 'independent' today than I would have been had I never left India in 1971. Regardless of whether one considers me a 'writer' cr not, I suppose I carry the brand name "expatriate." It was as an expatriate writer that I was asked to articulate some thoughts. What's more, I was given the luxury of allowing my thoughts to range any which way.

I will therefore dwell on the idea of independence, not because I feel shackled or constrained in any way in my chosen land, Canada. On the contrary, my family and I enjoy an easy life, have friends in all segments of North American life, and return to India every so often. But my fugitive Indian personality haunts me incessantly. My ambivalence towards my own so-called independence – that carefully wallpapered cornerstone – spills over into my ambivalence over India's independence itself.

I do not know if this is another unconscious attempt at rationalization, but I tell myself that, in the euphoria of an act of celebration, it is not uncommon to lose sight of what precisely it is that is being celebrated. The fiftieth anniversary of India's independence seems one such occasion. If independence means an end to an epoch of subservience under imperialism, then India undoubtedly won a great triumph in 1947, and some have every reason to once again celebrate that triumph fifty years later. But if independence means a chance for individuals to "grow" as they would wish to, to chart their destinies through the nagging chaos of everyday life, then it is doubtful whether there is too much to celebrate. In a similar vein, I find myself stopping short of exuberance as I look around my somewhat careless lawn, my landscaped backyard, and my spotlessly middle-class neighborhood. Have I truly survived what I left behind, I ask myself?

Survivors are rarely content. In life, as in war the survivor's joy is never wholly unfettered. There is always the memory of those who never made it. I am keenly aware of the arrogant and patronizing overtones of my last statement, as I know many friends' and family members who never for a moment regret "not having made it." They may regret the pollution, the high cost of living, the political corruption, but I have never heard them regret not having made it to America. My presumptuousness mocks me.

The troubling notion of independence will not let me be. I remember how, on August 15, 1947, I was a seven-year old, full of excitement and awe, in a seething mass of thousands waving tricolour flags and shouting 'Jai Hind' at the top of our voices. The rally of which I was a part was held in a vast space called Gandhi Maidan in the heart of Patna, close to which there once flourished the ancient city of Pataliputra, capital of the kingdom of Magadha. There was a real sense of history in the air. I remember my father, a doctor, and my uncle, an university professor drawing analogies with the glory days of Magadha and the Emperor Ashok – in terms of what lay ahead for the country. It was on this field that I was privileged to catch sight of Mahatma Gandhi a few months before his assassination, and about six years later, Pandit Jawaharlal Nehru.

On that day of August 15, 1947, I was too elated and too young to be concerned about the distant fires and cries of mobs I had seen and heard from the rooftop of our house in Bankipore only weeks, perhaps nights, before. These were the religious riots, and Bihar had its fair share of this horror. As I grew older and we routinely celebrated other "fifteenth Augusts", I was filled with a profound sadness as it dawned upon me that the joyous celebration of August 15 masked an enormous human tragedy, the Hindu-Muslim riots that tore apart Punjab, Bengal, Bihar, and many other regions that lay in between.

This simple ambivalence about a great historic event has turned increasingly complex over the years. I am often tempted to ask myself whether the event – often described as "a struggle of epic proportions", or "a triumph of the forces of non-violence" – was truly one or the other. No doubt there were elements of a vast, unequal struggle between the most powerful imperialist power of the twentieth century and segments of one of the most impoverished nations of the period. No doubt there were heroic personalities who led the struggle for India's independence. But I realize that a mere span of fifty years hardly allows one that perspective of historical understanding which would allow India's independence to be seen as a truly epic event.

And yet, every nation must have its myths and legends.

They are essential for a historical understanding of 'how things happened', essential for the primal need to know who we are. Other nations may laugh at these myths as unreal and fantastic, but the people whose forebears feature in these sagas often believe implicitly in the details, to the point of invoking the texts and critical junctures in their life-birth, marriage, death, and other occasions in between.

Two of India's great epics, the *Ramayana* and the *Mahabharata* are ritualized monuments to greatness and heroism. Ironically, the events out of which both these epics arose are about tragedy, about what happened when *dharmic* rules were violated. Petty family disagreements in the *Mahabharata* turned into a bloodbath of vast and unprecedented proportions. The *Ramayana*, on the other hand, deals with usurpation and fidelity. The tragedy that ushered Indian independence contains many of the elements of our two great epics. And always, after a bloodbath, after someone's victory, there follows a painful period of reconstruction and reconciliation. Nehru was right when he declared in a radio broadcast on the eve of independence: "The burden of foreign domination is done away with, but freedom brings its own... burdens...."

This brings me back to my own burden and the unconscious myths we 'fabricate' in our minds to justify our decisions and actions, and those of others. As a Canadian of Indian origin, involved as an academic in the study of the Asian sub-continent, and as a publisher engaged in the dissemination of the culture of that region, I should have been delighted by *The New Yorker's* coverage of India (June 23 and 30, 1997). Instead, I was profoundly disappointed. It was not Rushdie's predictable camaraderie with rising or shining stars of the Indian literary scene that upset me. Nor was it Amitav Ghosh's moving but very partial account of the 'other' fight for independence that left me uncomfortable. It was the casual superficiality, the cliches and stereotypes, and most importantly, the inadvertent but coldblooded butchery of the historic wholeness of the Indian subcontinent – the total marginalization of Pakistan and Bangladesh that I found unbearable.

The fact that *The New Yorker* was billed as a "fiction issue" seemed no excuse for parading the standard line-up of beggars, charlatans, greedy medical graduates, defecators on the river-bank, etc. All this is very amusing, but it is also old hat, and rather insensitive and insulting. It is sad that *The New Yorker* never really transcends this one-dimensional collection of the subcontinent's literature. This happy, feel good attitude is perhaps more commercially viable than a more introspective one. Pity, all we are left with are new versions of Rikki Tikki Tavi and the Indian rope trick.

The reason why there are suddenly so many Indian novelists is hardly a declaration of independence, as claimed by *The New Yorker* editorial. It is a manifestation of self-analysis, a sort of therapy for survival in a Darwinian global village where market forces determine the status of creative outputs. What gets published remains a function of neo-colonial instincts (or, simply put, the publisher's gut-feel reinforced by the dictates of marketing executives), and who gets published is a verdict, not on artistic integrity, but on how well one's sensibilities have been sharpened by colonial benchmarks of education and perception.

As an expatriate writer who was not photographed with Rushdie, Vikram Seth, and Arundhati Ray, my comments may well be construed as sour grapes. But I am certain it is more complex than that. I seem to be living with ghosts from my past. They are like hyenas ripping apart the carcass of my personality. I find little consolation in the fact that cultural dislocation is not restricted to me alone, but is a phenomenon affecting many in Indian society as well. As I reflect over the heroes of the independence movement, I realize that the Westernization of the East is a process of cultural change that neither Nehru nor Jinnah appeared too keen to resist. The continuing rumours about Jinnah's love for ham sandwiches and whisky derive from and sustain such rumours. Only Gandhi remains steadfast in his uncompromising values. In Gandhi's

Autobiography, he writes about a brief infatuation with English culture, as he calls it, in a section entitled "Playing the English Gentleman":

> Meanwhile my friend had not ceased to worry about me. His love for me led him to think that, if I persisted in my objections to meat eating, I should not only develop a weak constitution, but should remain a duffer, because I should never feel at home in English society. When he came to know that I had begun to interest myself in books on vegetarianism, he was afraid lest these studies should muddle my head; that I should fritter my life away in experiments, forgetting my own work, and become a crank.

This friend made one last effort to reform Gandhi. He invited Gandhi to go to the theatre, and to dinner at the Holborn Restaurant before that. Gandhi writes:

> The first course was soup. I wondered what it might be made of, but dared not ask the friend about it. I therefore summoned the waiter. My friend saw the movement and sternly asked across the table what was the matter. With considerable hesitation I told him that I wanted to enquire if the soup was a vegetable soup. "You are too clumsy for decent society," he passionately exclaimed. "If you cannot behave yourself, you had better go. Feed in some other restaurant and wait me outside." This delighted me. Out I went. There was a vegetarian restaurant close by, but it was closed. So I went without food that night.

We learn that Gandhi briefly turned to dancing lessons, French, and elocution. He even invested three pounds in a violin and something more in fees for music lessons. Before long, he wrote to be excused from further elocution lessons, bade goodbye to dancing, and went personally to the violin teacher with a request to dispose of the violin for any price it would fetch. In Gandhi's own words: "...I told her how I had discovered that I was pursuing a false ideal."

After more than twenty five years in the West, I would be less than honest if I didn't admit having asked myself the same question time and time again: Have I been pursuing a false ideal? There is also an interesting letter written by Indira Gandhi to

Nehru in 1947, shortly after she and her husband, Feroze Gandhi, had moved to a house in Lucknow. "It's such a nuisance not having a phone", she complained to Nehru shortly after moving in. "What a peculiar deadness there is in our provincial towns. And what makes the atmosphere sickening is the corruption and the slackness, the smugness of some and the malice of others. Life here has nothing to offer...middle-class young men. It is not surprising that the superficial trappings of fascism attract them in their tens of thousands. The R.S.S. (Rashtriya Svayamsevak Sangh) are gaining strength rapidly. They have been holding very impressive rallies in Allahabad, Cawnpore, Lucknow – except for very minor details following the German model....Are we inviting the same fate to our country? The Congress organization has already been engulfed most Congressmen approve of these tendencies. So do government servants." Only a few weeks later, one of those young Hindu fascists, Nathuram Godse, assassinated Gandhi in New Delhi. I ask myself once again if it is this I have been running away from the deadness of provincial towns, the corruption and the slackness, and emerging right-wing fascism.

It is regrettable that neither Nehru, nor Indira Gandhi or Rajiv Gandhi, ever fully appreciated that the economically disadvantaged in the late twentieth century appear increasingly to have found a refuge in religious bigotry. It gives them power. Not power that you pull out of a wallet, but power that comes from the spirit, however crushed and mutilated it may be. And that is a power not to be trifled with!

But others are running away, are we not? One possible answer to my question may be found in "Cowpath to America," a brilliant article in the *New Yorker* (June 23 and 30, 1997) by Abraham Verghese. Verghese writes:

> One morning, the visa officer turned down six consecutive doctors and told the seventh, who happened to be a friend of mine, and whom I'll call Vadivel, "Spare me the crap about coming back with specialized knowledge to serve your country. Why do you really want to go?" Vadivel, who had held on to his Ameri-

can dream for so long that he could speak with the passion of a visionary, said, "Sir, craving your indulgence, I want to train in a decent, ten-story hospital where the lifts are actually working. I want to pass board-certification exams by my own merit and not through pull or bribes. I want to become a wonderful doctor, practice real medicine, pay taxes, make a good living, drive a big car on decent roads, and eventually live in the Ansel Adams section of New Mexico and never come back to this wretched town, where doctors are as numerous as fleas and practice is cutthroat, and where the air outside is not even fit to breathe." The consul gave him a visa. The eighth applicant, forewarned, tried the same tactic but was turned down.

Portrait of a fellow-traveller, I ask myself? Those who can, are running away. Is it desperation, greed, rootlessness, or a loss of idealism that is driving Indians -- often the country's most valuable resources – away from their homeland?

Cultural change, and the cross-fertilization of cultures, appears unstoppable in this day and age, except by dictatorial decree. But must we, must I, run like lemmings along a path which earlier, and more frequent, travellers are having second thoughts about? Sociologists tell us that every new social construct contains the germs of the past. But what if the past becomes unrecognizable, and the present only causes us distress? Fifty years after India's independence – and twenty five years after my own -- my distress and that of the vast majority on the Indian subcontinent are all too palpable. These are the millions who have slipped through the cracks of development, who have been wandering aimlessly in the margins of two independent nations for the past fifty years. Meanwhile, a handful of others crisscross the COWPATHS, not only to America, but Canada, Australia, England, and anywhere else accessible to money.

It seems too fanciful to call ourselves members of the 'global village' and then imagine that the plague raging in one corner of the village will forever be confined to that corner. The cancer of poverty, corruption, confusion and rootlessness that afflicts the

Indian subcontinent appears to rage with equal ferocity as a cancer of the spirit in the 'developed' nations of the world. There is no escape, no exit. The Cowpath to America leads eventually to a gilded hell.

But I will return to my writing, my fractured self and all. And in spite of all my ambivalence and confusion, I will cherish my daughter's beautiful gift.

4

Crisis of Unbelonging in Some Expatriate Stories from the Canadian and Indian Context

P.A. Abraham

> Imagine a country as this country is, peopled by characters who have abandoned their setting and who seek to plot their own story in a new way. They choose to displace themselves, to surrender the familiar....Curiously enough, because they make the choices, they are happy, if not always satisfied with their story, and the effects of displacement only begin to appear in the children or grandchildren. Some people would say that it is only a matter of adapting to a new environment, or adjusting to a custom, of learning a language. I maintain that it is much more profound , a displacement so far-reaching that it only vanishes after several generations....I learned that the world was fiction and fiction was refuge.
>
> Aritha Van Herk

The above quoted words by Dutch Canadian novelist, Aritha Van Herk evoke well the challenges not only of writing as an expatriate but also of reading.

Nowadays, many use expatriation and immigration as synonyms. However, it is important to draw a line of demarcation between the two though that line is a thin one. As the term implies, expatriation focuses on the native land that has been left behind, while immigration denotes the country into which one has ventured as an immigrant. According to Stainslaw Barnezak, the words "exile" "emigrant" and "expatriate" are sad prefixes that conjure up "states of exclusion" (16) However, he points out that the excluding "e" has its opposite in , as in immigrant or inclusion. In other words the expatriate lives on his "ex" status while the immigrant celebrates his present in the new country.

Today, in postcolonial literatures "the expatriate sensibility" has been accepted as a legitimate literary term. The impulse to take the literary journey home, towards "history", towards "memory", towards "past" is the result of the expatriate's long journey from home. Faced with rejection, the expatriate clings to his ethnic identity. Irwing Howe has identified nostalgia as the real reason for the expatriate's need to evolve ethnic origins(174).(Personally, I consider 'ethnic' to be a derogatory term. The expressions 'mainstream' and 'ethnic minority' should be replaced by 'ethnic majority' and 'ethnic minority', as these terms imply a more balanced and comprehensive framework for Canadian life and which can be meaningfully related to the historical and social reality of Canadian society).

Caught between two worlds, the expatriate negotiates a new space, caught between two cultures and often languages, the expatriate writer negotiates a new literary space. Therefore, an anxious sense of dislocation is characteristic of expatriate writings. The shifting designation of 'home' (Where's it?) and the attendant anxieties about homelessness and the impossibility of going back are perennial themes in these stories.

George Steiner describes the expatriate writer as "the contemporary everyman". It is also described as a state of mind and emotion which includes a wistful longing for the past. It is often symbolised by the pain of exile and homelessness. There is a complex view of the double vision of the expatriates-both a looking forward and a yearning backward. It is, in fact, part of every person's life, it is part of the human condition. No matter where you lived, even if you lived in the same place all your life, you would look at the past, at lost moments, at lost opportunities, lost loves.

This paper is an attempt to explore the dilemmas of displacement as faced by Canadian expatriates and Indian expatriates in some of the stories of Mavis Gallant, a Canadian expatriate writer living in Paris, and Bharati Mukherjee who had emigrated to Canada, married a Canadian writer Clark Blaise and now residing in the US, respectively.

Gallant had spent her formative years in bilingual Montreal and briefly in English-speaking Ontario. Speaking as an insider and as someone who has lived outside the country for a long time, she views Canada always from a distance, as Canada remembered elsewhere. Gallant does not invariably write about Canadians, about one third of her stories are about Canadians, while others are about Australians, South Africans, Americans and Europeans displaced by the war. But her collection of short stories, *Home Truths* (1981) consists of stories only about Canada.

"The Ice Wagon Going Down the Street" is a story about Canadian expatriates for whom 'expatriation' has become a way of life, a state of mind where optimistic dreams of living in the future balance against a condition of being permanently lost. Peter and Sheilah Fraizer, husband and wife had moved away from Toronto to Paris in the early 1950s and are now back in Toronto from the Far East in the 1960s with their two daughters staying as guests in the house of Peter's sister.

> 'Everybody else did well in the international thing except us'
> 'You have to be crooked,' he tells her
> 'Or smart. Pity we weren't'(107)

There isn't much that happens in the story. But in the process of narration, layerings of dream and pretence and loss under the Fraziers' faded glamorous international image, are successively revealed.

The title of the story indicates an old-fashioned provincial world far removed,it would seem, from the Frazier's mode of living. Yet as Peter and his wife Sheilah sit drinking coffee on a Sunday morning in Toronto dressed 'like peacocks' in their silk dressing gowns from Hong Kong, the morning dissolves into Peter's memory of someone else's remembered morning, a different kind of Canadian morning where a girl from a poor expatriate family in Saskatchewan had watched 'an ice wagon and a trail of ice water in a morning invented for her" (134). Peter's memory of that girl, Agnes Brusen, and their discreet encounter in Geneva is the one secret he keeps from his wife, and the image of the ice wagon had lodged in his mind as the sign of a precious fleeting moment of shared recognition between them. Of course, Agnes was mislaid when the Fraziers moved on once again from Geneva to Ceylon. But strangely the memory Agnes had entrusted to him surfaces on another morning in a different place after many years and it slowly enters into Peter's vision of his own failure and loss. The story ends on a note of tension between his 'true Sunday morning with his wife in Toronto' and his sense of guilt and failure:

> No, begin at the beginning. Peter lost Agnes. Agnes says to herself somewhere, Peter is lost.(134)

The story which consists of disparate memories, is structured on a powerful opposition between two images: the ice wagon of Agnes's secret life and the Balcenciaga dress which belongs to Sheilah. Nothing belongs to Peter. The ice wagon is also suggestive of the freshness and promise of a prairie morning for a young girl and the black Balanciaga afternoon dress suggesting an increasingly soiled relic of a wonderful past. According to Coral Ann Howells, it is also suggestive of "the values of 'home' in contrast to the Balenciaga, the symbol of... Frazier's failed aspirations" (96). Here, Peter is caught between cultural values and he becomes an exile.

The phrase 'dislocated for ever' occurs in another story, "Virus X" which is about two girls from Winnipeg who come to Europe on a Royal Society scholarship. Lottie Benz is working on her sociology thesis "the integration of minority groups without a loss of ethnic characteristics" (178) and Vera Rodna has been "shipped abroad to an exile without glamour" (176) because she was pregnant. In the story there are two different Canadian responses to Europe. While Lottie Benz, resisting the challenges Europe offers, goes back to Canada, Vera Rodna decides to stay in France. Eroding the differences between the two characters, the narrative reaches the point where new choices are possible for them. Lottie had the opportunity for self-realization in France, but she chooses a safe return to a married life in Canada. So the story ends in betrayal of friendship and her own self. Lottie will have to forego so much and there is again no guarantee that her assimilation will be successful.

Lottie's attack of illness in Strasbourg from the mysterious 'Virus X' is important in the story. Diseases and damages occur frequently in Gallant's stories and they have direct relationship with the psychological and emotional crippling of her characters. Lottie's disease generates her flashes of insight. Only in that state of disease that she realizes the futility of her thesis as no sociological theory can truly account for the complex variety of human relationships and in this state she realizes that her experiences in Europe have transformed her immensely: "She was dislocated, perhaps forever, like the clock in Strasbourh Cathedral" (204). Though these are her feelings in her delirium, these have connections with an experience in Strasbourg while travelling to meet Vera. It was during this time that Lottie for the first time spoke German in public. It is 'the secret language' of her family and her childhood memories so defensively hidden under her image of Canadian respectability. Those German words release certain 'warm memories' of 'home' – not of Winnipeg but of an almost forgotten ceremony "never mentioned as German, never confirmed as Canadian" (189). But Lottie keeps all this secret from Vera for "none of this was Vera's business" (190). It looks as though all Lottie's important realizations are enclosed in her mind, like the revelations of real experiences in her imaginary letters to her fiancé in Winnipeg, or her view across the plain of the Rhine, that ancestral place "she loathed and craved, and never mentioned" (195). In short, all real feelings are situated in the private space of her mind. Even Vera's recklessness can only stimulate a momentary response in Lottie.

Their important point of togetherness is the celebration of Vera's twenty first birth anniversary at a cafe in Strasbourh. While returning "drunk on friendship" they meet Lottie's fiance waiting for them in the hotel lobby. For a moment, Lottie knows what their future will be like:

> One day, she would become accustomed to Kevin, Lottie said to herself: stop seeing him, as she had nearly grown used to mountains.(211)

But she feels terribly insecure and frightened and she makes her choice by telling a lie:

> What I would like, Kevin – I don't know if you'll think it's a good idea – would be to go back with you. If I stay here I'll get pneumonia. Its a good thing you came. Vera was killing me. (213)

When Vera packs her bags and leaves for Paris, there is nothing for Lottie to do but to get ready to go home with Kevin. Lottie does two odd things before she leaves. She "made a list not of what she was leaving behind: food, wilted anemones, medicines, all Vera's residue as well as her own" (216). Instead her farewell gesture to Strasbourg is her last imaginary letter to Kevin, which was "not a letter to anyone. There was no sense to what she was doing. She would never do it again. That was the first of many changes" (216). Lottie decides to carry out her original determination stated to herself on her arrival in Paris:

> She intended to profit from this winter of opportunities.... but in no sense did she desire to change or begin a new life.(175)

But there is a curious undermining of such certainties as the narrative moves from indirect interior monologue to the voice of the omniscient narrator in the last sentence, "many changes?" (216). Lottie did not expect any changes when she arrived in Europe. But she was forced to face changes in an alien atmosphere. "There was no sense, to what she was doing" is indeed ambiguous. The sentence is in response to her writing of the imaginary letter. But does it also refer to her final departure (as the list making and the letter might suggest)? But oné thing is sure that she feels a terrible sense of loneliness.

As stated earlier, expatriation is also a state of mind whether one is in one's own country or in an alien land. Gallant's story "Orphans' Progress" is an example. This is a story about the growing up of two sisters Cathie and Mildred. They are orphans living in Montreal after being taken away from their French Canadian mother at the ages of six and ten because she was branded by social workers to be unfit to care for them. First they are moved to their father's mother in Ontario, then to their cousins in Montreal, then to a convent, and eventually Mildred is adopted by another aunt and her name is changed. When the sisters meet again at the ages of fifteen and nineteen, they feel no sense of relation and do not know what to say to each other and they are incapable of any emotional responses. This is yet another kind of solitude, where "not knowing" changes from being the happy condition of childhood innocence shared by the sisters to the emotional paralysis of the two young women entirely damaged by their upbringing. The story ends with Mildred's point of view as she looks at the garage where she and her sister had lived very happily with their mother:

> Mildred glanced up and then back at her book. She had no reason to believe she had seen it before, or would ever again.(62)

Of the many signs of emotional trauma suffered by these girls, the most obvious is the change of language involved in their "helpless migration" from Montreal to Ontario and back to Montreal again. While in their grandmother's house "French was an inferior kind of speech" and in Montreal,

> Language was black, until they forgot their English. Until they spoke French, nothing but French, the family pretended not to understand them, and stared as if they were peering in the dark. They very soon forgot their English.(60)

As Coral Ann Howells points out,

> The result of such linguistic quandary is not only the separation between words and their meanings but also a split within the self and 'forgetting.(101)

In her introduction to *Home Truths*, Gallant says:

> ...memory is something that cannot be...ordained. It can, however, be destroyed, and it is inseparable from language.(xv)

While Mavis Gallant deals with 'Canadians abroad', Bharati Mukherjee's characters are mostly 'Indians abroad' especially in North America. Hers is a classic example where one can mark a clear change from expatriation to immigration. For a writer like Bharati Mukherjee, writing is a political act. Her personal sense of marginalization as a woman, a woman of colour, and as an expatriate/immigrant makes her vent out her feelings so vehemently in her stories.

In Canada, Mukherjee claims to have experienced racial discrimination. In *Days and Nights in Calcutta.* (1977) she describes her agonizing experiences in Canada owing to her paradoxical position of being "both too visible and too invisible"(169). While her colour made her too visible, as a writer she was invisible. She observes in an essay entitled "Immigrant Writing: Give Us Your Maximalist":

> I was a psychological expatriate, though a naturalized Canadian for fifteen years, simply because Canada is a country officially hostile to the concept of assimilation.(It proclaims the virtue of its multicultural policy).Perceiving myself to be in a comfortable but unwelcoming environment, I struggled to maintain various emblems of my difference.(50)

Mukherjee considers expatriation as a restrictive and self defeating attitude in a writer. The expatriate writer is always in a mood of complaint and projects the pain of exile and becomes a figure of solitude.

In an interview with Alison B.Carb, Mukherjee talks about her personal trauma in Canada and the hostility towards Indians in Canada. To quote her again:

> ...the attitude in the sixties and seventies was that if one hadn't played in snow and grown up eating oatmeal one didn't have anything relevant to say to Canadian readers. The seventies were horrendous for Indians in Canada. There was a lot of bigotry against Canadian citizens of Indian origin, especially in Toronto....Toronto made me a civil rights activist. I wrote about the devastating personal effects of racism....(651-652)

Mukherjee's early novels *The Tiger's Daughter* (1971) and *Wife* (1975) explore the conditions of being an Indian expatriate in North America. The protagonists of the novels Tara and Dimple respectively are expatriates, geographically as well as in mind and spirit. As any other expatriates, they too are not comfortable in both the native and alien cultures. Here expatriation is not only a major theme but also a metaphor for deeper levels of solitude and alienation.

As mentioned earlier, an immigrant plunges into the present new world. An immigrant undergoes an important change in the process. The so called assimilation involved in immigration, however, does not mean a denial of the past, which is an impossibility. It probably means giving up a rigid hold of the past. It is a recognition of duality or in the words of Mukherjee, a recognition "of fluid identity". In her introduction to the collection of stories *Darkness* (1985), Mukherjee says that she saw her Indianness not "as a fragile identity to be preserved against obliteration,...but as a set of fluid identities to be celebrated" (3)

I shall discuss three stories from *Darkness* which, according to Mukherjee are written in Canada and they are purely "Canadian stories", "uneasy stories about expatriation"(2). They are "The World According to Hsu", "Isolated Incidents" and "Hindus".

In "The World According to Hsu", Ratna, of Indian origin and her husband Graeme Clayton, a Canadian professor of Psychology at McGill University, Montreal, are on a holiday at an island off the coast of Africa. It is said that he went there to see the southern cross and to persuade Ratna to move from French dominant Montreal to English dominant Toronto where the

University had offered him the chair in Personality Development. Ratna prefers Montreal, because there she was merely 'English' that is an English speaking Canadian, not even Indian. She would be called a "Paki"(41). Three incidents of violence are reported. Just before going out to see the southern cross, Graeme casually informs Ratna that he has accepted the job in Toronto. Her fear and insecurity are contrasted with his cool indifference. He goes all alone to see the stars while she reads the label on the wine bottle 'Cote de Cassandra'. The name may be symbolic of the Cassandra vision of doom. Though she is ignored by her husband, she acquires the knowledge of her expatriate existence.

The story "Isolated Incidents" depicts a Canadian's attitude towards an expatriate. the Canadian Ann Vane's job is to file complaints from immigrants on problems concerning Human Rights. Two specific cases of racial discrimination in Toronto are brought to her notice – that of Miss Supariwalla and John Mohan Persawd. Ann Vane's detached view of the cases is tinged with irony. She is aware of the futility of documenting such cases:

> Torontonians were proud of their subway, their politeness, proud of their moral spotlessness. This after all was not New York. Attack on John Mohan Persawd and dozens like him would always be considered isolated incidents and not racial.(82-83)

In "Hindus", written in Canada, but set in America, Mukherjee juxtaposes an expatriate against an immigrant and brings out the contrast quite vividly. The narrator of this story Leela Lahiri represents Mukherjee's concept of an immigrant's "fluid identity". She proudly proclaims, "I am an American citizen"(133). At the same time she is also proud of her Bengali Brahmin ancestry. H.R.H Maharajah Patwant Singh of Gotlah is an obvious expatriate with a grievance against India. When Leela and the Maharajah meet after two years, the Maharajah is writing his memoirs. While the Maharajah narrates his woes,

Leela celebrates her new identity as an immigrant.

However, Leela does not deny her Hindu past; she accepts her dual existence.

In the rest of the stories and in her next collection *The Middleman and Other Stories*, Mukherjee's characters are energetic immigrants and one can very clearly mark a definite movement away from expatriates to immigrants who are in fact middlemen in more than one sense.

The world of the stories of Gallant and Mukherjee is fragmented. Their characters often live in a world of nostalgia, centered on a sort of homesickness, bearing the pains of uprooting and re-routing, the struggle to maintain the difference between onself and the new unfriendly surroundings. Mukherjee's "Indians abroad" seem to have developed a feeling of inferiority complex and also a sense of refusal to accept the identity/non-identity forced by an alien environment. They also seem to be more self conscious and inhibited than the "Canadians abroad". Both are torn between the old and the new world values. The stories do not give any solutions for the problems faced by these expatriates. They just point out certain crucial moments in their lives and that moment is indeed a moment of revelation or as James Joyce who was also an expatriate called it "epiphany". Joyce's *Dubliners* also raises similar problems regarding the questions of detachment and uncertain distance between the narrator and the characters. There are no authoritative interpreters in the stories except the narrators. A.J.Gurr has identified this sort of narrative detachment as the clearest hallmark of the exile (34). This is also a characteristically modernist stance shared by Eliot and Joyce.

The journey motif is adopted in almost all stories, a journey from one country to another, from one place to another, from one time to another, from one solitude to another. In fact the motif is the controlling pattern of these stories and it is circular. The journey is more clearly the essential form of these stories because it represents in physical terms an approximation to their themes. The persistent resolve to make a fresh start in life functions as the silent centre of these stories.

As stated earlier, there seems to be no solution for the problems faced by the expatriate. The only solution probably the reader can conjecture is to accept the fact that all expatriation/emigration involves anxiety and belonging to two communities which forces a kind of struggle with something other people do not have to struggle with. That growth is painful, but that is part of the expatriate experience. In other words, it is a recognition of doubleness, "fluid identity". It is an acknowledgment of alternative realities. This I feel is a positive way forward, where we take from each other's cultures and redefine our hopes and aspirations. After all, culture is not a static thing. It constantly moves.

References

Baranczak, Stainslaw. "Confusion of Tongues" *Writers and Writings*. 16-18. Feb.6, 1969.

Carb, Alison B. "An interview with Bharati Mukherjee". *The Massachusetts Review*, Winter 1988-89.

Gallant, Mavis. *Home Truth: Selected Canadian Stories*. Toronto: Macmillan, 1981.

Gurr, A.T. *Writers in Exile: The Identities of Home in Modern Literature*. Sussex: Harvester, 1981.

Howe, Irving. "The Limits of Ethnicity". *Ethnic America* ed. M.Weiser. New York: The H.M.Wilson Company, 1978.

Howell, Coral Ann. *Private and Fictional Worlds*. London: Methuen. 1987.

Mukherjee, Bharati. *Darkness*. Canada: Penguin Books, 1985.

—. "Immigrant Writing: Give Us Your Maximalists". *The New York Times Book Review*, Winter 1988-89.

—.*Days and Nights in Calcutta.* New York: Double Day and Company.1977.

5

"Hahnji" means "Yes, sir": Reading Sameness and Difference in Canadian Writing

David Stouck

In a study of Canadian literature titled *Oppositional Aesthetics*, Arun Mukherjee argues that universal standards dehistoricize and depoliticize literary texts. Her argument is made in much the same spirit as when Chinua Achebe wrote famously "I should like to see the word universal banned altogether from discussions of African literature until such a time as people cease to use it as a synonym for the narrow, self-serving parochialism of Europe" (11). In writing about Canadian literature, Mukherjee is particularly determined to insist that "no universal criteria can be worked out that will apply" across cultural differences (17). At the heart of Mukherjee's argument is the claim that an historical and apolitical Anglo-American canon makes room for only certain kinds of writers—those from the white, chiefly middle-class, English or French speaking segments of Canadian society—and for only certain kinds of literary subjects—chiefly, the individual hero's quest for self discovery, or the individual's effusions over the beauties of nature and anguish over mutability. What is eliminated, she argues, is the communal point of view, and the social, political themes of history, specifically those of conquest and subjugation, racism, sexism, and class conflict.

I would concede at once that there is much truth in Mukherjee's charge—the western literary critic has for a long time put the individual at centre stage—but to call for all literature and criticism to issue from the point of view of community and social-political life is equally an extreme position, one which does violence to works of literature where an individual's experiences and memories are foremost in importance. One can read any work of literature in terms of its socio-historical context certainly, even writers like Jane Austen or Henry James whose fictional worlds seem hermetically sealed off from the economic and political realities of their time; but to stop there would be as limiting as reading a novel by Salman Rushdie in terms of the psychology of one character rather than in terms of community life and its historical transformations. To find a middle ground that recognizes the existence and value of certain universals, but where local interests, particularly cultural differences, are also cultivated, I will turn to thinking about mode and language and how these essential components of a literary text constitute the reader's need for experience that is both familiar and unique.

Mode is a way of describing motivation in a work that is not contingent on time or place, that remains stable across the centuries and from culture to culture. It provides a basis from which we can relate to the experiences of people who lived hundreds of years ago or in totally different cultures at great distances from our own. One can identify four different modes. Briefly, *romances* are stories of individual adventures, those quests for self-discovery that Mukherjee feels have usurped the western imagination for too long, while *pastorals* embody the individual's experience of remembering and sometimes grieving. *Satires* and *epics*, on the other hand, serve the communal interests, epic celebrating the history of a community or nation, satire criticizing its practices and exposing its shortcomings.

In Canadian literature readers from other cultures can identify with the experiences of coming of age described in the romances of Ethel Wilson, Margaret Laurence, Sinclair Ross, or Howard O'Hagan (*Tay John*). Stories of escape from oppressive family or social situations, choices about the future that involve career and a mate, where and how to live—these have a universal currency. Pastorals, or memories of growing up in a specific region, have helped in the meantime to create a literary map for Canada: Alice Munro in rural Ontario, Ernest Buckler (*The Mountain and the Valley*) in the Maritimes, Gabrielle Roy in Manitoba, as examples. Writers from minority cultures have continued this same imaginative mapping of Canada by remembering what it was like to grow up outside the Canadian mainstream: two recently-acclaimed books are Vi Plotnikoff's *Head Cook at Weddings and Funerals* (1994), about a girl from a Russian Doukhobor community, and Wayson Choy's *The Jade Peony* (1995), about being a boy growing up in Vancouver's Chinatown. Another twist to this kind of story in Canadian literature is the story of growing up in another country—outstanding here are Michael Ondaatje's *Running in the Family* and Anita Rau Badami's *Tamarind Mem*. These are both books about individuals who are returning in memory (and in Ondaatje's case by means of physical travel) to the places of childhood to examine and understand better the sources of personal unhappiness. Ondaatje is haunted by memories of a father he never got to know, and Badami tells us of a mother who was remote and sharp-tongued with her children. Both narrators live in Canada and assess their childhoods from that distance. Badami situates her mother's unhappiness—and in turn her own—in the context of arranged marriages. But Ondaatje simply describes a flamboyantly mismatched couple who eventually divorced and left their children emotionally and to some extent physically adrift. Not to consider the psychology of the narrators in these fictions and the textures of remembering would be to overlook the real motivation behind the writing.

There has also been a lively tradition of *satire* in Canadian literature: Thomas Haliburton, Stephen Leacock, Mordecai Richler, Robertson Davies. Much of it has been conservative, whereby the eccentric individual is laughed at or scorned and the practices of society as a whole reaffirmed. The speaker in

Davies' *Fifth Business* would seem to be highly critical of the world around him, but it would be misleading to see him as making radical judgments, because the values he affirms are both elitist and traditional ones. There are some important exceptions to this strong vein of conservative satire: poets like Earle Birney and F. R. Scott, a dramatist like George Ryga (*The Ecstasy of Rita Joe*), and a writer like Margaret Atwood, in all her generic guises, have positioned themselves outside the mainstream of society and from that vantage point they want Canadians to see the limitations of the society they have created, to feel uncomfortable with religion as coercive rhetoric, with prejudicial attitudes to race, and with rigid constructions of gender. And these are, of course, the goals shared presently by satirists around the world.

Mukherjee is correct in lamenting the absence of the communal point of view in Canadian literature; the epic mode has seldom been voiced because historically there has not been a strong sense of nation building nor, until recently, a sense of a people oppressed. Epic in an abstract and literary fashion is present in the long poems of E. J. Pratt which celebrate phases of the nation's development: the heroism of the Jesuit priests in *Father Brebeuf and His Brethren* and the building of the transcontinental railway in *Towards the Last Spike*. It is there in a muted way in Pauline Johnson's *The Legends of Vancouver* where she transcribes a local chief's oral myths for a literate European audience. These epic legends are framed by nostalgia for a way of life that is quickly vanishing, but there is no anger or resistance to what is happening. Those feelings are conveyed rather much later by a European writer, Rudy Wiebe, whose novels *The Temptations of Big Bear* and *The Scorched-Wood People* are written in anger against what the white settlers did to the native peoples on the prairie. But the best epic written in Canada by far—a loser epic—is a novel called *Pelagie* by Antonine Maillet. This book tells the story of the French-speaking Acadian people who were deported to the southern United States by the English in the 18th century and how they slowly made their way back to Nova Scotia and New Brunswick. But most Canadian writers working with epic material have chosen to write pastorals instead, memory books about the injustices their people have suffered. Joy Kogawa's *Obasan*, for example, tells of the disenfranchisement and relocation of Japanese-Canadians during and after the Second World War, but the story is told from the point of view of a remembered childhood. But, however Canadians have chosen to tell their stories, mode allows connections across cultural boundaries.

In the particulars of language, on the other hand, we confront difference and recognize the importance of local interests. An interesting way to consider how literary texts make us experience other cultures is through language which is not completely translated for us by the author. In the Anglo-American mainstream, writers can assume their readers always know what they are referring to, even when they write from specific places like the American South or the English west country, but in works of multicultural literature (works in English from Third World countries) and in the literature of smaller countries like Canada, regionalisms and local references occupy a different status in terms of intelligibility. Reed Way Dasenbrock argues that the political meaningfulness of a work of literature from a foreign country resides in the amount of work the reader must do in order to understand what a book is saying. Only by doing that work, he says, by striving to understand a different way of speaking, are we brought up against the fact of cultural difference. If everything is translated into our terms and made readily accessible, then our cultural categories will be reinforced rather than challenged. This is nowhere more evident than in a writer's use of names and words that are totally alien to the Anglo-American reader. A reader opening the pages of a Rohinton Mistry book experiences this very quickly-words such as *gunga* (cleaning lady), *dhaba* (kitchen restaurant), *goondas* (ruffians), *yaar* (buddy), *tamasha* (fair), *Hahnji* (Yes, sir), and lines of speech like *O babu, ek paisa dayray*! (sir, can you spare a penny)

-- they are there at the beginning of Mistry's books without translation or full explanation, partly to accustom us to another way of life, but also because they can't be fully translated, they are different and that difference must be acknowledged. We can translate *Hahnji* as "Yes, sir" and recognize the speaker's address as being respectful, but the non-Indian reader probably does not hear very clearly the conditions of class or age that necessitate that respectfulness, which can stretch from the honorific to servility, that is, the socio- economic position of the speaker. Here I would argue is a crucial centre of a work's meaning in terms of its international audience. Mistry is very aware of his audience. The international reader is everywhere inscribed in Mistry's texts; for example in the way he describes at length in *Such a Long Journey* Parsi religious customs, prayers, costume, and funeral rites at the fire temples and the Towers of Silence. But in untranslated words such as *dugli, Behram roje, dustoor, navjote*, there is not only cultural distinctiveness asserted but a resistance of the Parsi to conform or identify with the logocentrism of either the British or the Indians. The hybridity of Mistry's use of two separate discursive strategies can be read as a political act---to claim and preserve cultural territory for the Parsi. At the same time the use of specifically Parsi words has a nostalgic function of resituating the speaker in his childhood in Bombay. The Parsi idioms then temporarily de-center the English reader from his or her own culture -- insist on cultural difference -- yet simultaneously they centre the reader in the universal experience of pastoral recollection.

We might ask: how have Canadian writers created a middle ground between universal themes and the particulars of the Canadian experience? Our earlier writers, in fact, did little to create a middle ground for Canadian culture. Some of the early, popular ones exploited all the stereotypes of what is Canadian: Ralph Connor wrote about the Mounted Police, Pauline Johnson about the noble redmen, William Henry Drummond about the French Canadian habitant, and Robert Service about the snowy frontier. Later, more serious writers, effaced all markers of Canadian identity from their work – writers like Morley Callaghan whose moral parables are set in some nameless city, or Sinclair Ross whose early stories and famous novel, *As For Me and My House*, never mention Canada or Saskatchewan, or any locale other than the symbolic Horizon. The same is true for Sheila Watson in *The Double Hook*. Frank Davey, in writing about the Ross novel, has said such texts speak from a position of marginalization and silence. Ethel Wilson, publishing a little later, was also reluctant to ask her readers to do the kind of cultural work I am describing here. But her way of serving the reader is opposite to what I have mentioned so far. She writes of her Canadian setting all the time, but she assumes her reader has not heard of British Columbia or Vancouver (or knows very little of them, or is disinterested) and takes pains to give detailed information about the place. For example, she opens "Lilly's Story" in *The Equations of Love* by telling us that "In the early part of this century there lived in the young city of Vancouver in British Columbia a large family by the name of Hastings." And a few sentences later we are told about "the soil and moisture of the British Columbia climate which encourages weed and flower, tree and vegetable with almost tropical energy." The reader of *Swamp Angel* will recall with what pains the author describes the topography in both the city and on Maggie's journey into the interior of the province of British Columbia.

It wasn't until the late 1960s that Canadian writers began to refer unapologetically to a Canadian setting, making interested readers actively take part in learning about the country and its culture. The novels of Rudy Wiebe are about the native peoples of Canada in complicated and demanding ways, and poems by Margaret Atwood about a figure like Susanna Moodie or, more recently, her novel Alias Grace about an Ontario woman jailed for murder in the mid-19th century make large demands on the reader to know something about Canadian history. Robertson

Davies, Margaret Laurence, Alice Munro all write about Canada as a place they expect their reader to have some background knowledge of.

But this need for background knowledge becomes even greater when reading books from Canada's minority cultures, and as we have seen with Mistry the use of unfamiliar, foreign language is often an index to how much a writer expects a reader to cultivate that middle ground where mainstream and minority can meet. Sometimes it is not very demanding: in *Head Cook at Weddings and Funerals* Vi Plotnikoff is very conscious of the reader who knows no Russian, but she wants to preserve certain words as being more evocative than any translation could render them, so the Russian words are there—words like *babushka*, *padrushki*, and *angleeki* -- some of them translated in appositive phrasings, others not, and invariably it is the ones not translated that make us feel the difference, not the explanations that Doukhobors like to chew sunflower seeds, or that they were pacifists, and so on. Similarly in *The Jade Peony*, Wayson Choy's Anglo-American readers encounter strange words (*lo fan* words) and meanings that are an untranslatable part of Chinese culture; to preserve the character of intimate family relations the Chinese names are retained. But there is one word especially where the engaged reader must change his or her way of seeing things. Choy describes growing up surrounded by ghosts. The Anglo-American reader thinks of a ghost as a spirit, as a haunting inanimate presence, but the text makes clear this is a reference to a white, non -- Oriental person, a very animate and corporeal presence. The effect, however, is to show the reader a way of using this word and seeing the world in a way in which that distinction between a spook and a white person is not made. Anglo-Americans experience a different perception and a category of thought when confronted with this word in this text, and in so doing learn a good deal about Chinese perceptions of the 'Other.' The insistence on new perception through use of alien words (what Bakhtin would call dialogical language) grows ever stronger and declares itself now in titles: in her residential school diary, Shirley Sterling asserts her native identity by calling her book, *My Name is Seepeetza.* An even more challenging title is *Tamarind Mem* by Anita Rau Badami, where neither word is immediately intelligible to a non-Indian reader.

The best of cross-cultural criticism also mediates between the local and the universal. Anjali Bhelande's recent study of Ethel Wilson and Indian philosophical thought describes parallels between Wilson and various Indian thinkers that show both sameness and difference at once. Mystical texts from India, secular fiction from Canada, and yet both are joined by many philosophical threads: self and other, being the other, involvement in humankind—Indian philosophical issues being explored in the social issues preoccupying a 1950s woman writer in North America. Universal standards narrowly defined in terms of theme may indeed serve only parochial interests, but the human imagination as understood in terms of mode eludes such boundaries, is inclusive, and connects varying peoples. And language, articulating histories, engages readers in making those bridges between cultures specific.

References

Achebe, Chinua. *Morning Yet on Creation Day.* Garden City: Doubleday, 1976.

Bhelande, Anjali. *Self Beyond Self: Ethel Wilson and Indian Philosophical Thought.* Bombay: S.N.D.T. Women's University and Bharatiya Vidya Bhavan, 1996.

Dasenbrook, Reed Way. "Intelligibility and Meaningfulness in Multicultural Literature in English." *PMLA* 102, 1987.

Davey, Frank. "The Conflicting Signs of *As For Me and My House*" in *From the Heart of the Heartland: The Fiction of Sinclair Ross*, ed. John Moss. Ottawa: University of Ottawa Press, 1992.

Mukherjee, Arun. *Oppositional Aesthetics: Readings from a Hyphenated Space*. Toronto: TSAR Publications, 1994

Wilson, Ethel. *The Equations of Love*. Toronto: McClelland and Stewart, 1990.

6

Identity Crisis of Indian Immigrants: A Study of Three Novels

Shyam M. Asnani

Though the writer's individual talent should be rooted in the tradition of a particular society and culture, the real strength of the modern literary imagination lies in its evocation of the individual's predicament in terms of alienation, immigration, expatriation, exile, and his quest for identity. Culturally and even linguistically estranged as the individual feels about himself, the whole question of his social, emotional, ethnic or cultural identity assumes mythic proportions and thus becomes an unattainable ideal.

One can argue that identifying differences within a culture is not the same as using systems of categorisation that in effect retain existing differences as though they were natural and good. In the first case, difference serves to invigorate a culture, keeping it alive; in the second, difference simply preserves a static distribution of social power. The first is egalitarian, the second hierarchical. The first opens opportunities for change, the second operates as a catalyst for keeping cultures apart in the name of tradition, but with the effect of validating one tradition over another.

This paper seeks to examine how identity dilemma finds its articulation in three contemporary novels: Kamala Markandaya's *The Nowhere Man* (1972), Bharati Mukherjee's *Wife*

(1976), and M.G.Vassanji's *No New Land* (1991) in which the protagonists of Indian origin are uprooted from their moorings and are expatriated to alien countries. All the three novels are tragedies of bicultural experiences in their gruesome aspects.

The contemporary literature which deals with emotional problems clearly reflects the pathetic condition of the modern man. Getting uprooted from the native cultural traditions and values, the loss of indigenous language, man's position as a mere outcast or an unaccommodated alien, together with multiple injuries and lacerations of the psyche, all account for the theme of 'identity atrophy' in these three novels.

The Nowhere Man opens with Dr Radcliffe diagnosing Srinivasa's disease as leprosy which is symptomatic of his physical and emotional ostracism. Thrown into an alien land as a stranger, he is condemned as an 'unwanted man'. In the structure of the novel is woven the past life of the protagonist, and with the help of flashbacks the novelist highlights the cultural clashes both in his homeland and in the country of his adoption.

Wife is also about displacement and alienation, for it portrays the psychological claustrophobia and the resultant destructive tendencies in that condition in Dimple Dasgupta – a young Bengali wife who is sensitive enough to feel the pain, but not intelligent enough to make sense out of her situation and breaks out. Dimple is entrapped in a dilemma of tensions between "American culture and society and the traditional constraints surrounding an Indian wife, between a feminist's desire to be assertive and the Indian need to be submissive." No resolution can possibly emerge from the subversion exercised by the values – ideals of freedom, and individuality identified with America, and the cultural identity – Dimple's – that they undermine and unravel.

No New Land unfolds the story of Nurdin Lalani and his family, who in the 1970s, have been uprooted from their native land and transplanted to the new world of the Toronto suburb of Don Mills. Much to their chagrin, their dreams of the new land are shattered. Nurdin is haunted by his old world values. Failure to find a decent job adds to his misery, and one night as he returns home, he is shocked to know that he is being implicated for allegedly assaulting a girl. Though ultimately he manages to come out clean of this stigma (with the legal assistance provided by Jamal, another immigrant), Nurdin has to reconcile himself as a 'marginal man' whom fate has decreed to live in two worlds and in two not merely different but antagonistic cultures.

As the narrator of *Shame* muses: "What is the best thing about migrant peoples...? I think it is their hopefulness... And what's the worst thing? It's the emptiness of one's luggage... We've come unstuck from more than land. We've floated upwards from history, from memory, from time" (Rushdie 1983: 87). The three writers under discussion need to 'journey' home not only to satisfy a nostalgic impulse but to reclaim the past and to recreate a collective history and myth of their peoples. Often they write as the 'Other', alienated by racial and cultural differences. This results in a 'resisting', 'fighting', 'protesting' literature, leaving an insidious impact on the complacent conformity of the canon.

Apart from nostalgic reminiscences, a more serious consideration, however, can also be perceived in the writers' act of recreating the past. They thus become folk historians, mythmakers, and custodians of the collective history of their peoples. In many instances, as Vassanji states, "this reclamation of the past is the first serious act of writing. Having reclaimed it, having given himself a history, he liberates himself to write about the present" (Vassanji 1989: 63-67).

Since the immigrant writer speaks from the margins, his focus is off-centred. Likewise, his protagonist hardly ever takes centre-stage, because it is not 'his-story' that is being narrated. Instead, the narrative gives voice to community life, to local or national politics, to the experience of being alienated, obscured, peripheralised, and marginalised. The quest motif, which seems the archetypal pattern in the literature of the predominant mainstream culture, and which is also conceived in terms of a metaphoric and sometimes an actual voyage, undergoes here a sea change. As Arun Prabha Mukherjee points out, "the artist-as-hero creating in the isolation of his soul" type of protagonist is nowhere to be seen. Here lies instead, "an encounter with history and hence with one's otherness" (Mukherjee 1989: 48).

In a survey of South Asian Canadian Literature, significantly entitled *A Meeting of Streams*, Uma Parameswaran (1989: 80) argues that instead of the keyword assimilation, acceptance of diversity as mutually enriching is a necessary tool for cultural synthesis – a direction in which literature can play an important role; since "... literature not only reflects persistence and change in society but can lead society into a better appreciation of its multicultural and ethno-centred fabric."

Excepting for its aboriginal population, Canada is peopled by immigrants from across the globe. To speak of Canada hence is to speak of a nation made up of many nations. In other words, it is like an "ocean fed by many a river in which flow the tears and joys of its seventy or so cultural groups." (Suganasiri, quoted in Hutcheon & Richmond 1990: 9). Despite Canada's policy of promoting multiculturalism officially pronounced in 1971 and further reinforced in the Bill C-93 of 1988, the mainstream- centred discourse still continues to be the hegemonically dominant power structure. The paramount question, the writer writing from within a particular culture-specific consciousness which is labelled as ethnic or immigrant, inevitably comes to grips with is: "How do you write in a new country?" In regard to the larger problematic of establishing the Canadian identity, Kroetsch (1983: 88) lays stress on the choice of the appropriate narrative mode: "The very ability to see ourselves is based on the narrative mode: the I telling a story of I, of we, of the they that mirror us."

Since Kroetsch's proposition emanates from his awareness of being a part of the margin, it assumes greater significance for the ethnic/immigrant writer situated identically within Canada.

Like Kroetsch, he too must confront the poser: What kind of story is the ethnic/immigrant writer going to tell? He has two broad choices: he can either write about Canada like mainstream writers do, and thus try to be like 'them'; or, he can write about his ethnic world and thus be different. While the first choice sounds pragmatic in terms of wider reading audience and greater opportunity of book sales, it contains the inherent danger of providing an outsider's superficial, insufficient vision or one which is stereotypical. The unnamed narrator's internalization of the American ethos in Atwood's *Surfacing* would be irrelevant in the case of ethnic writer's simulation: "If you look like them and talk like them and think like them then you are them" (Atwood 1983: 139). He may approximate them, but he just cannot be them – how do you dye your skin white? In his stubborn zeal to disguise himself as them by renouncing all that is his -- his inherited culture, beliefs, language and sensibility, he would risk being a "free floating... citizen of the world" (Atwood 1982: 113). On the other hand, if he writes about his own ethnic world from his inherited ethnic consciousness, he imperils himself of being ghettoized and discriminated against as a marginal figure on the Canadian literary scene (Salat 1992: 3).

If one were to specify what the novel *No New Land* is about, it is about the ethnic/immigrant minority group of tenants at Sixty-nine Rosecliffe Park Drive in Don Hills whose lives dramatize the little ironies, the pathos and the hardships of having to live between two worlds neither of which promises hope of stability and happiness. As the narrator comments, "You try different accents, practice idioms, buy shoes to raise your height. Deodorize yourself silly." On the one hand is the persistent memory of "home" which Haji Lalani, Nurdin's father, and Missionary fondly recall as they sit on a bench in Dar and gaze at the Indian Ocean. On the other is the recurrent and pervasive sense of futility captured in the epigraph, a quote from "The City" by C.P.Cavefy:

> There's no new land, my friend, no
> New Sea; for the city will follow you,

In the same streets you'll wander endlessly.

Most of the characters live in the hi-rises in Don Mills, where the security of the numbers provides an illusion of "homes" and shelter from an alien and unwelcoming society. The narrative voice ironic and detached, strikes the right balance, as the novel records a wide range of incidents, most of them poignantly pinpointing the sordid spectacle of racism, prejudice, hostility and ruthless marginalization. And yet the referentiality is simply one of the variegated aspects of the novel which lift the narrative beyond documentary, beyond the preoccupation with the quotidian (Kanaganayakam 1991: 57).

In a memorable scene, responding to a question by Missionary that the plastic goddess in the lobby of the hi-rise draws attention to the absence of a male god, Nurdin leads him to the window, points to the C.N.Tower and says: "There is our god. But he is a deep one Mysterious." The Tower veritably is a pervasive presence in the novel, often described in mock-religious terms that foregrounds its function as a symbol of "Amarpur", the promise of paradise, which always remains elusive. The juxtaposition of the Tower and the plastic goddess points not only to a dichotomy between the religious and the secular but also to the dualities that threaten one's identity, and to the values that refuse to thrive on alien soil (*Ibid.*).

The flashbacks dealing with life in Dar evince that the novel is as much concerned with the past as the present. Patterns of repetition, such as Haji Lalani being slapped for looking intently at a German woman in Dar and his son later being accused of raping a woman in Toronto coalesce the past and the present, the private and the public. Similarly, the incident of Nurdin's puritanical father whipping Akbar for writing a letter to Sushila juxtaposed with Nurdin being tempted by Sushila in Toronto (who, coincidentally lives in the same neighbourhood as the girl who accuses Nurdin of molesting her) suggest a deliberate undermining of the realism of the novel. The synchronic structure, as Kanaganayakam (1991: 57) observes succinctly, steers the novel away from the present to the past, to areas of experience that lie beyond the immediate referential context.

Early in the novel, the narrator comments:

> We are but creatures of our origins and however stalwartly we march, paving new roads, seeking new worlds, the ghosts from our pasts stand not far behind are not easily shaken off.

The past finds expression in the puritanical Haji Lalani, whose religious fanaticism and blind adherence to an iron-discipline instilled by the colonizers terrify the children, compelling them either to leave home or to internalize a sense of guilt. Nurdin, in particular, is tormented by his repressed guilt, and his marginalization in Toronto is in part a consequence of his past. It takes Missionary, a revered Ishmaeli figure from Dar, and a repository of communal wisdom, to exorcise Nurdin's past, heal his bruised feelings and give him hope for the future.

The endings of the three novels examined in this paper have a rich complexity and symbolic suggestivity.

Though married to an educated and liberated husband, Dimple is not able to strike a balance between the two juxtaposed worlds: the one she left behind and the other she has come to live in. She is so much frustrated with life that the use of words like loyalty, suffering and pain, on her husband's part, have lost meaning and instead, she starts fantasizing the act of murdering her husband. She has already been in a sick state of mind ever since she left India, but the alienation from her husband, the environment, the sham and the outward glitter of American life drive her to the fits of psychic depression and ultimate insanity. The novel ends on a pathetic note, glimpsing a distraught woman who has become "impulsive, foolish... a maniac" (212), watching on T.V. women "getting away with murder" (213) and fantasizing her own husband's murder.

Vasantha in *The Nowhere Man* leaves behind the impression of a strong character obstinately rooted in her own culture and obdurately refusing to adapt herself to the 'alien land'. That she has treasured a handful of Indian soil and a bottle of water from the holy Ganges, the drops of which are sprinkled on her ashes, symbolically suggests not only the transformation of the Thames in the holy river but also the fact that she has an indomitable will and titanic spirit to zealously preserve her cultural moorings.

In Nurdin's case, when the charge of rape has been withdrawn, his innocence proved beyond doubt, and the past exorcised with the help of the missionary, he feels an urge to "take on the future more evenly matched" (207). He must now think of his family and his job. He is not going to let a mere embarrassment rob him of the security the job brought him to. He becomes resolute to face the odds bravely. The experience of the charge of rape brings about a complete metamorphosis in him and makes him aware of his own potential worth. The novelist symbolically uses the red fez of Haji Lalani to free him from his fear and sense of being unwanted, and the C. N. Tower now goads him on to the new path of his life-in the new country and the new culture. Rather than returning to the old idea of home, he now becomes aware of the new realities which have to be accepted, and in them and through them, he must come to grips with himself.

No New Land is a seminal postcolonial novel that foregrounds the voice of the margins without apology or rancour. Problematizing our perception of nation and identity, it compels a reassessment of the standards that govern our vision of what constitutes the canon.

References

Atwood, Margaret. *Second Words: Selected Critical Essays.* Toronto: Anansi. 1982.

—. *Surfacing*. Toronto: General Publishing. 1983.

Kanaganayakam, Chelva. "Don Mills and Dar-e-Salaam" *Toronto South Asian Review*, 9, iii (Spring). 1991.

Kroetsch, Robert. "Beyond Nationalism: A Prologue." *Open Letter*. 5th Series (Spring). 1983.

Mukherjee, Arun Prabha. *Towards an Aesthetics of Opposition: Essays on Literature, Criticism and Cultural Imperialism*. Toronto: TSAR. 1989.

Rushdie, Salman. *Shame*. New Delhi: Rupa. 1983.

Salat, M.F. "Denying the Givens", Unpublished Paper at a Seminar, p.3. 1992.

Suganasiri, Suwanda. Quoted in *Other Solitudes: Canadian Multicultural Fictions*, eds. *Linda Hutcheon and Marion Richmond* (Toronto: O.U.P.). 1990.

Vassanji, M.G. "The Post colonial Writer: Myth Maker and Folk Historian," in M.G.Vassanji (ed.). *A Meeting of Streams: South Asian Canadian Literature*. Toronto: TSAR. 1989.

7

South Asian Immigrant Women Poets: Postmodernist Contexts

B.R. Nagpal

Multiplicity, ambivalence, inauthenticity are some of the marked characteristics of the South Asian immigrant women poets whose attempt at self-definition is to be validated by their geographical-cultural-racial-political contexts. Reality, therefore, is perceived as utterly fluid insofar as the real unreal overlap, negate, affirm. These paradoxes and the shifting, fleeting time space sequence, social specifics in terms of class, gender, are reflected in the feminist outpourings of these women poets. It may be pointed out, therefore, that the diverse voices of these poets which is a facet of Canadian mosaic, multi-culturalism provides individual, literary, dialogic nature of the articulation of their complex, elusive experience. The evocation of new reality is the outcome of every indistinct self grappling with the unintelligibility in its singular manner so that the modes of perception, verbalisation are notable for their distinct difference.

Despite the fact that these poets hail from different regions like India, Bangladesh, Sri Lanka, the historical nature of their predicament like their sense of marginalisation, search for roots is uniquely akin to one another. Their visualisation of their experience and the concretization of the immediate in radically different idiom is indeed a process towards the relocation of their identities. The discursive nature of consciousness, quest for an idealized vision and the sense of inadequacy, incompleteness obtrudes upon the psyche of these writers who are apprehensive of their logic and regress to their sub-conscious fears of racial persecution, imperialist exploitation, white manipulation and a sense of self-annihilation. However, the smokescreen of these negatives is consistently subject to change so that the newly discovered truths make imperative positive possibilities. In a cryptic statement made by Bakhtin it has been pointed out how limited reality is capable of stretching itself and being more expressive. Bakhtin writes, "The unfinished nature of self is not mere subjective licence; like any border it is also a limit....In the realm of culture, outsideness is the most powerful factor in understanding" (Holoquist 26).

The expatriate writer whose mode of operation is subject to the memory of the past, confrontation with the present and receptivity towards the future is continuously drawn towards the need for an integrative world which does not denote hegemony, racial class solidarity but an organic connection between the subjective self and the objectivised narrations that complement one another in the newly traversed paths. It is in this context that Linda Hutcheon eulogizes the struggle, challenge and the craft of Canadian writers who confront contradictions but are "governed only by compromise and kept strong only by moderation" (Hutcheon 332). The sense of uncanny bewilderment, therefore, is not an abysmal hell-state for these writers who are consistently discarding dying old identities in terms of sabotage, subversion, disorder, racial prejudice and are reliving with newly born selves that are activated and seek a sense of wholeness in their meaningful, viable exploration. The knowledge of a recognizable self, and an autonomous identity is a projection of trans-continental consciousness when repressions, and delusions about the past are to be erased or overcome.

The problem for the immigrant women poets like Uma Parameshwaran, Surjit Kalsey, Lakshmi Gill, Himani Banerjee, Suniti Namjoshi is not one of schizophrenia or dual reality but one of affirmation and re-affirmation in a new perspective. The sense of release, freedom experienced in a new environment may present juxtaposed polarities between the indigenous culture and the culture of their adoption but the racial-historical-political equivocations are to be supplanted by the cravings of a new self, new equations that denote adjustment, order harmony and solidarity. The new world presented is not a fantasy that cancels the reality of the past but on the contrary is a readjustment, adaptation, participation and fulfilment.

Diana McGifford's incisive comments about the nature of vocation of these poets in her "Introduction" to *Shakti's Words* are worth quoting "She is us, but a little newer and fresher, and her poems are a little more honest than ours. If she has found a country our country has found a poet". The evident suggestion is that these poets pursue an emerging landscape, visualise a scenario in which they are being conditioned and shape their utterances in language and images that signal an end to the catastrophic blockages. The sense of resistance and openness to new frontiers of reality implies transvaluation of categories and concepts. The frame of reference is one that is a pointer to the newly surcharged self that has a different connotation, a different ontology where the determinants like race, ethnicity, political, historical, sexist ramifications prove ineffective.

It may be pointed out how the acknowledgement of a new self in the poems of Uma Parmeshwaran points to the realisation of a territory that has literary and cultural evocations. The following statement of the poet elaborates her viewpoint "Every immigrant transplants part of his native land to the new country and the transplant may be said to have taken root once the immigrant figuratively sees the river that runs in the adopted place, not the Ganga or the Assiniboine as the Ganga, both of which imply a transference or substitution - the confluence of any two rivers in sacred" (79-80). She has also remarked in the same vein, "Canadian literature, we hope, will extend its front and expand its vocabulary in order to accommodate the university of our multi-cultural reality" (80). The poet's poems like "Usha" "Demeter I miss you", "A Wedding Song" point to the mediating consciousness that enacts the dramatisation of selves trapped between the sense of home and the new environs only to resolve into self fulfiling area of activity where there is a sense of belongingness and participation. The poet's utterance in "Usha" is as follows:

> Rejoice, for though I am gone, the imprint of my hands is on the crumbled wall and on these hanging waters, bound each to each through me. (McGifford 70)

Usha counsels a path of self-amendment and self-acknowledgement. In another poem, "A Wedding Song" the accent is on accommodation, the uplifted resurgence and the experience is epiphanic. The lyrical lines of the poet are as follows:

> We who had seen winter come suddenly
> had turned up our thermostats
> and driven in gas heated cars
> along the frozen river, our Assiniboine
> . . . . .
> Had only distinctly thought of the lonely swirling
> of her warm waters locked under ice unending. (McGifford 72)

Evidently, the suggestion is that Ganga and Assiniboine are sanctified icons of fertility and the two archetypes cannot be substitutes for one another but can exist as correlatives.

The existentialist sense of void that the trauma of dislocation engenders can only result in a temporary sense of helplessness, but eventually the public avowal of private grievances melt into the ebullient spirit of self- acceptance that points to an encompassing order. Himani Bannerjee in her poem, "Paki Go Home" expresses her indignation against the dominant group of Whites and finally seeks the dissolution of her discords in a psychological-philosophical stance on her sense of oneness. The poet's outburst is as follows:

> Even the child in the womb
> must find a voice
> sound in unison

organise
Like a song, like a river
like a prophecy that changes the world. (McGifford 6)

The plausible, realizable truth for an immigrant poet cannot flow from an existentialist sense of non-being, anxiety, guilt, narcissism, and over protectiveness. The fancies and the irretrievable stages that some of the poets weave around themselves in their state of political expediency as also group subjugation is a regrettable stage. The moral and spiritual retrieval for these poets provides an allegorical streak in South Asian immigrant poetry when the ensnaring web of alienation, self-loss, reductiveness is over-shadowed by a sense of reconciliation. Surjit Kalsey expresses in the poem "Voices of the Dead":

I don't know/when the earth/was shattered
within me/I can recall the moment/when
I turned to a stone. (McGifford 59)

The awakened sense of synthesis, meaningful alternative is presented in another poem, "A Woman with a Hole in Her Heart"

Don't tell me
Woman is a woman - a mistake of nature,
a rib of Adam or a broom, a mop or anything else
She blooms like the first crux of the Universe,
The glory of all created existence. (McGifford 58)

Lakshmi Gill is another significant representative voice of the panorama who in her self-reflective outbursts makes palpable her sense of apathy, delirium replacable by rejuvenated self, hope and resilience. She writes in one of her poems, "Light Canada":

And yet I remain
Looking at the dust
and at the bay
as though this land
would disembowel
its profound secrets. (McGifford and Kearns 25)

The sense of derelict skepticism or other variables of her poem "Beneath the Purple Lantern" that makes the poet discern spiritual bliss in future. The self exalting tone of the poem is as follows:

Suffer the loss of this generation for the next
suffer suffer suffer
Behold the Crucifixion and the glorious Resurrection.
(McGifford and Kearns 36)

Undoubtedly, there are poems when the poets discover their psyche as afflicted, an inverted state that lends credibility to their state of aggression, nausea and nostalgia. Suniti Namjoshi in one of her poems, "The Beasts Came up to Me" expresses her frantic deviations in the face of imperious assaults:

Any moment now the fabric would tear;
Someone would say I had no business there
And I could get up and either fight or run.
(McGifford and Kearns 57)

In the absence of any definable essence, the South Asian Immigrant woman poet confronts her border-line stage as an apprehensible relative truth. Such a state bristles with challenge. The sense of the unconciliatory in the poets gives rise to overstatement, understatement, irony, banality and rhetoric. However, the existentialist sense of relationship involves knowing yourself through the Other who makes significant presence. Sartre's words are pertinent: "I recognise that I am as the Other sees me. There is, however, no question of comparison between what I am for myself and what I am for the other" (Silverman and Elliston 161). The implicit suggestion is that even when the poets ruminate over their state of dehumanization, colonialism and racism they wrestle with themselves to figure out meaningful postures so that their metaphysic of solidity is not negative but a stage in the process of affirmation and concurrence. The dubious foldings of their situation only unravel for them a luminous stage where their being is definable.

It may appear, therefore, that a poet like Uma Parameswaran discovers herself rooted in an alien land where the exotic, romantic references, repressions are replacable by the inward rhythm of her delineated reality, her poetic vitality and her contemplative sweep that does not bracket objects and persons but on the contrary makes them relational. Parameswaran's poems are attempts to view reality in totality, fuse glory with decay, myth with sordidness in order to communicate the sense of a unified being and an orchestrated sense of living experience. In her poem, "Chandrika", Parameswaran writes:

> My heart contracted and exploded in fear
> But I reached up to the alcove our shrine
> as I had the day before
> and I gave him the last
> of my sealed holy water. (McGifford and Kearns 76)

Evidently the poet's world is one of re-activiation, humaneness, exuberance and is self liberating

The clogged fears and oppositional stages can either be brushed aside or the claustrophobic world of subservience may prove dismal so that a sense of fragmentation, paranoia turns out to be hammerings towards a sense of self-oblivion. Thus when there is an existentialist sense of personality definition, the contradiction is one of an acute sense of depersonalization. The mock self-assertion in lesbianism and feminist moorings are obvious modes of release. Kaushalya Bannerjee in one of her poems "Insomnia" construes in the following vein:

> i must deconstruct you
> in myself, the hardest
> most unwanted task
> piece by piece
> cell by beloved cell.
> i take you apart
> and reassemble you (Bannerjee 58-59)

Nilamberi Singh communicates her distinctly sexual self in the following lines of the poem "To Two Moral Selves."

Where loving you becomes more virtuous,
Then does my daily pile of unwashed laundry.
(McGifford and Kearns 90)

Such an experience may sound like a crisis of consciousness, but once it becomes a facet of the transmuted world of the South Asian immigrant woman poet, the sexual reality can only point to change in the offing. Surjit Kalsey strikes a kindred note in one of her poems, "Siddharth Does Penance Once Again" where her utterances strike an indefinable life-mystery.

I've begun to do penance
denying my emotions and feelings
I've begun to search for
the other salvation this time. (McGifford and Kearns 42)

In an ethos of unpredictability where an overwhelming sense of the indeterminate is experienced by an inarticulate self who consistently delves within, the South Asian immigrant woman poet yearns for otherness, registers several tracks in her journey towards self-fulfilment and self-enrichment. The emancipated psyche encounters distortions within itself when power-structures give way to new constructions. The impressions communicated by various poets are an evidence of intermediate stages and interdependent worlds so that no external reality can impose itself from outside even at the heightened sense of dissolution. Every reality is a constituent of the unknown greater reality that has its unknown constructions. It is this quality of the South Asian women poets that lends them their mystique and makes their prose reverberations so piquant.

References

Bannerjee, Kaushalya, "Insomnia", *Toronto South Asian Review*, Spring Vol. X. No.3

Holoquist, Michael, *Dialogism: Bakhtin and his World*, London: Routledge and Kegan Paul. 1990.

Hutcheon, Linda " As Canadian as Possible under the Circumstances" *The Canadian Essay* eds. Gerald Lynch and David Rampton. Ontario: Pitwan Ltd. 1991.

McGifford, Diana. Ed. *The Geography of Voice* Toronto: TSAR, 1992.

McGifford, Diana and Kearns, Judith, "Introduction", *Shakti's Words* Toronto: TSAR, 1993.

McGifford, Diana and Kearns, Judith. Eds *Shakti's Words*. Toronto: TSAR, 1993.

Parameswaran, Uma. "Ganga in the Assiniboine: Prospects for Indo: Canadian literature", *A Meeting of Streams*. Toronto: TSAR, 1985.

Silverman, Hugh J. and Elliston, Frederick A, *Jean Paul Sartre: Contemporary Approaches to Philosophy*. Pittsburgh: Duquanne University Press, 1980.

8

On the Borderlines of the Present: Temporal Strategies in Mukherjee and Mistry

Rajul Bhargava

Let us begin by 'essentializing' the very act of writing. The first premise is that all writing entails a certain *generalized system* which is in constant negotiation with specific instances which could either be events (socio-political) attitudes (politico-economic/social) or psychological spills (psycho- sexual). It is these specificities that help in actuating self definition by combining the parts to the *whole.* The parts are the 'past' – individual or particular and historic; they are things that happened, a collection of 'axioms in a socius', which give cultural self-representation and thus become the symptomatic central contents for the larger diagnostic whole which is the generalized system – the *real* present, which is actually the remaindered, the essential use value part of the past.

The second premise is that all writing depends on a pre-existing code and to conceive of a 'living present' one must understand that there was a 'present' before and that there will be a 'present' after. It is this that makes for continuity. If the present 'before' i.e. the past is missing, the work will be a monstrosity and if the present 'after' is not there it will be an anachronism. This continuity can be transitional or transactional, if the former it makes for cohesion and a lineal configuration leading to writing with a chronological sequencing. But if it is the latter (transactional) it is ramifying, more often than not circular, oscillating between the present and the past. It is not only continuity, but discontinuity as well which is subtly meaningful.

From writing let us move on to actual life. It's laws of time cannot be tampered with, they are beyond human alteration. We can never live tomorrow today, or live yesterday tomorrow or refuse to live *ab novo* or skip or re-live events. But when life is being transcribed into writing the narrative imagination can defy the tyranny of time and decree impossible calendars in which the future can precede the present and the past can follow the future; in which time begins *in medias res* and is punctured with gaps, and events repeat. The narrative imagination is an ingenious existential outlet of escape from the iron rule of linear time where call the "defamiliarized designs of deformed time illuminate the hidden meaning of time which eludes ordinary consciousness restricted by the familiar way of time".

The familiar way of time is the chronological continuity the lineal equivalence of events. It is an idea that historicism proposes and which, most commonly, signifies a people, a nation, or a national culture as an empirical sociological category or a cultural entity. But once this signification disappears as in expatriate narratives which are without a national culture, an added parallel dimension, a duality of time, a temporality of representation is needed that moves between cultural formations and social processes without a centered causal logic. Homogeneous visual time must be dispersed and if we are to give the nonsequential energy of lived historical memory and subjectivity its appropriate narrative authority, we need another 'writing time' which can be no other than the borderline of the present, a time without duration: the vertical paradigm of diachrony replaced by the horizontal syntagym of synchrony.

The expatriate writer occupies a marginal or a borderline position, he sits on the periphery of the past, causing the future to take shape. If he recedes into the past his works would have the value only of a memoir, a travelogue or perhaps of an autobiography – all being limiting since they are subjective, personalized. If on the other hand the writer chooses to completely assimilate himself into the new culture he ceases to capture the sympathy of the people in the homeland who in a way sustain him, keep him alive (isn't expatriate writing mostly bought/sold 'at home'?) since sympathy in the host culture is a far cry. So the expatriate writer on the borderline of the present does a tight–rope walking, keeping up a stance of double talk, with a show of simultaneity, coalescing the past with the present to recreate a future.

This present, the contemporaneous, in such cases takes on the responsibility of conveying the "accumulative scraps, patches and rags of the past" and also weaving them into the texture of the future. These pre-given (the events, attitudes or psychological spills) help, as said earlier, in actuating self-definition, self-representation, without which the present would be reduced to a meaningless void. And so it is the past which diagnoses the present. This present can be seen as a glass or spectacle through which one sees everything, it is a point from which one articulates one's ideology (Althusser), the critique of causality (Engles), the materiality (Marx). It is not however the sum total but the remaindered, the essential use value, and therefore paradoxically the margins have to be cathected to define the center and the center is always constituted in terms of its marginality – so the past is essential in constructing the present time.

Having thus defined the 'present' in expatriate narratives, let us see how Bharati Mukherjee and Rohinton Mistry relate it to their "being" (before) and "becoming" (after). There can be two relational configurations in such narratives: the assimilatory and the disintegratory.

The former follows a characteristic paradigm beginning with restlessness, repression of the past and an overt acceptance of the present; the latter begins with a feeling of loss passing, through various shades of nostalgia and culminating into schizophrenia. Both Mukherjee and Mistry reveal an assimilatory consciousness. It can possibly be traced to their own individual disintegratory past where Mukherjee's public school, elitist status and Mistry's religious minority make it impossible for them to wholly relate to their larger nationhood. Moreover their expatriation was the outcome of their own choice, it was not thrust on them which made their assimilation easier, though not always pleasurable, i.e. rising to their desired expectations.

It is because of this discontinuity between the 'wish' and the 'wished for' which makes Bharati Mukherjee say that she feels betrayed. In "A Wife's Story" she writes:

> It's the tyranny of the American dream that scares me. First you don't exist. Then you're invisible. Then you are funny. Then you are disgusting. Insult, my American friends will tell me, is a kind of acceptance. No instant dignity....I long, at times for clearcut answers. Offer me instant dignity today, and I'll take it...I long for ugly rage. (*Middleman* 26).

But Mukherjee like her protagonist has been trained to behave well and instead of 'dignity' that rage would have given her, she only simmers inwardly, realizing that back at home things would have been different. A Mamet play in India, insulting foreigners, would have been safely locked up. It is not as if she has not been in control of herself, she has faced riots, uprootings, separation, her son's death... but this. In the effortless meanness of well-bred displaced, third world women, she vents her feelings: "You're exploiting my space". Time has taught her better, expatriation has made her more keenly aware of her nationhood.

Of course, she has broadened her horizons. She can even think of winking back at the cops when they "smile at her with benevolence". She wants to get them into trouble, wants to break into a dance. But her culture asserts that it would be "silly". And yet her decorous upbringing of the Anglican boarding schools is but a memory. Soon the memories of Indian destitutes mix with the hordes of New York street people, and (she floats) free rejoicing in the fact that:

> I've made it. I'm making something of my life. I've left home, my husband, to get a Ph.D in special ed. I have a multiple entry visa and a small scholarship for two years. After that we'll see. (*Middleman* 29)

For the present 'trucks' have replaced 'lorries' in her vocalbuary as has the host culture, the earlier part of her life is over. Even her husband on a few days visit gets coloured:

> He pulls me close, slips the straps of my nightdress off my shoulder.
>
> "Wait a minute."
>
> I wait, unclothed, for my husband to come back to me.... In the ten days he has been here he has learned American rites: deodorants, fragrances. Tomorrow morning he'll call Air India: tomorrow evening he'll be on his way back to Bombay. Tonight I should make up to him for my years away, the gutted trucks, the degree I'll never use in India. I want to pretend with him that nothing has changed.
>
> In the mirror that hangs on the bathroom door, I watch on the bathroom door, I watch my naked body turn, the breasts, the thighs glow. The body's beauty amazes. I stand here shameless, in ways he has never seen me. I am free, afloat, watching somebody else. (*Middleman* 40)

That is to say "free" of the *past*, "afloat" or assimilated in the current of the *present*, "watching" the reshaping of the *future*. The various forays and repeated reminiscences turn the past into a mythic concept of the mind where memories take on the shape of rumours.

In another story "The Tenant" Mukherjee sees the past, history, "as a net, the kind of safety net travailing trapeze artists of her childhood fell into when they were inattentive or clumsy" (*Middleman* 98). The break away from the past, the center, is again very obvious here in this story which is narrated from the borderline of the present. In the present the last names "which give ancestral secrets away" are to be avoided just as the idea of "borrowing". She always pays cash never 'borrows'. Even her "brahminness" doesn't seem to mean much to her:

> 'Brahmin' isn't a caste; its a metaphor. You break one small rule, and the constellation collapses. (*Middleman* 106)

Maya, the protagonist, has moved out of her Brahminic pale. She has "slept with married men, with nameless men, with men little more than boys, but never with an Indian man. Never" (*Middleman* 103). One may guess why; perhaps because "She has broken with the past. But." (102) The 'but' here is a loaded one, for even if she believes she has become an American citizen do the Americans take her for one? The past has not broken away from her; she has decentered herself but has not found herself another center. She is on the periphery, a mere onlooker. The strain of her tight-rope walking tells on her psyche, she wants to plant herself firmly, to make virtue physical. She longs to belong. She wants to escape from the "confused world of the immigrant", the "lostness". As a move to find meaning she takes a complex detour into time from the vantage of the periodicals room, an "asylum for homesick aliens". But it has an unsettling effect on her, it fills her with a familiar feeling of *longing*. She has changed her citizenship but she "hasn't broken through into the light, the vigor, the *bustle* of the New World. She is stuck in dead space." A temporal space of the present which is grim, perverse. Her leaving behind her "parents' ways", her "miraculous rebelliousness" has, made her accomplish nothing. We see Mukherjee moving in a stereotypical expatriate paradigm characterized by phases of restlessness, repression of earlier self, overt acceptance of the present – all in a flux. It is a kind of disjunctive temporality that she is faced with. What she is attempting to do is to narrativize contentions of the self which require her to look at the "belonged" past from the context of the "unbelonged" present, through an inherited vocabulary and inherited customs. Thus as life moves from one time to another, from one place to another, one way or the other, for one reason or the other, it gives a further perspective of her identity. The partitioning off, the reducing life into "now" and "then", "here" and "there" does make for a whole, but a featured, truncated whole.

Even the titles of the two collections discussed here, *Darkness* and *The Middleman and Other Stories*, are symbolic, which can be translated as temporal metaphors. *Darkness* takes us back into the past, the stories have a retrogressive effect, while *Middleman* converges towards the present, the borderline of the future. What the future holds is yet to be seen as Mukerjee hints in her 'Introduction' to *Darkness*:

> I see most of these as stories of broken identities and discarded languages, and the will to bond oneself to a new community, against the ever present fear of failure and betrayal. The book I dream of updating is no longer *A Passage to India* it's *Call It Sleep*. (*Darkness* 3).

Whether the book will accept "forced peace" or "thrust forgetfulness" is yet to be seen.

Rohinton Mistry too in *Tales from Firozsha Baag*, quoting Tagore, feels that "his house is all dark and lonesome -- lend me your light." The darkness is of the "closed past" and not "open present"; the "light" would come when he totally assimilates into the 'present' present. In the "Swimming Lesson" for example, the whole story is a kind of explanation on what happens when an expatriate tries to make a place for himself in the host culture and how he learns to handle his parent culture. The beginnings are always the most difficult when the "past" is really merged into the present and the writer is sent speeding back at the slightest pretext. The old man in the wheelchair reminds Mistry of his own Grandpa and he is filled with remorse for having treated him so shabbily: "I should have gone to see him more often". But what is the use of raking up the past when it is buried, dead as Grandpa.

After an interlude in which Mistry suggests that his tryst with his past is becoming as weak as his letters are becoming meager: "This is just a quick note to let you know I'm fine, so you won't worry about me. Hope everything is okay at home"

(232). So with "The sun is hot today" we are back into the present where he is getting acculturized. He looks long and longingly at the two women sunbathing in bikinis. He prays that the heat and haze might make them forget and so prolong their stay. His world of make-believe comes shattering down when on close quarters he doesn't find them as attractive:

> The elevator arrives and I hold it open inviting them in with what I think is a gallant flourish. Under the fluorescent glare in the elevator I see their wrinkled skin, aging hands, sagging bottoms, varicose veins. The lustrous trick of sun-and-lotion and distance has ended. (233)

As has also ended the infatuation with the new land and there begins the first discriminatory, derogatory onslaught: "Are you from India?" "Is swimming not encouraged in India?" Mistry is still raw to let an offense drop by, "On the contrary," he begins a justification. Just like all other moves to assimilate, the swimming lessons too end in a failure.

> Failure to swim through filth must mean something other than failure of rebirth -- failure of symbolic death? Does that equal success of symbolic life? death of a symbolic failure? death of a symbol? What is the equation? (240)

The equation is that a sterile attempt at being anything other than an Indian is more than fully compensated by making one's Indianness fertile material for creative productivity.

Whatever else Mistry failed at, he succeeded in obliterating the present by sitting on its very periphery.

"The leaves are beginning to fall" and as the first snow falls the past in covered up in inches of snow. The seasons have run a full circle. The "heat" has gone away altogether. The stories that were about "life left behind" now are about "the life to be faced".

> The last story they liked the best of all because it had the most in it about Canada, and now they felt they knew at least a little bit, even it was a very little bit, about his day-to-day life in his apart-

> ment; and Father said if he continues to write about such things he will become popular because I am sure they are interested there in reading about life through the eyes of an immigrant, it provides a different viewpoint; the only danger is if he changes and becomes so much like them that he will write like one of them and lose the important difference.(248)

Till now the difference is only performative. Then he opens a new can of Azax to scour all that had been soiled. Soon it will be spring and everything will change.

> The dwindled days of winter are now all but forgotten; they have grown and attained a respectable span. I resume my evening walks, it's spring and a vigorious thaw is on. The snowbanks are melting, the sound of water on its gushing, gurgling journey to the drains is beautiful. I plan to buy a book of trees, so I can identify more than the maple as they begin to bloom.(249)

Now the change is total "I wipe my feet energetically on the mat because some people are entering and I want to set a good example".(249)

This discussion originated in a concern for the aesthetics of narrative rhetoric and a feeling for time. It examined the configurations of time categorizing it not in terms of Order, Duration and Frequency however important they might be, but in terms of time as a mode of knowledge which enables man to negotiate with reality, with the problem of temporality, his time boundedness. The vivification of time in narrative rhetoric, specifically in expatriate narratives expels our diminished experience of time in actual life or virtual time and expands us to the truth of time. Above all, the artistic *gestalt* of time functions as a metaphor for a philosophy of time.

Note

Much of the terminology used in essentializing writing has been influenced by my reading of Derrida and Gayatri C. Spirak.

Notions of time and temporality are a take off from recent studies in narratology, especially of Gerard Gentle, Wallace Martion, Frank Kermode, Jerome Bruner, Peter Brooks and David Lodge.

References

Mistry, Rohinton. *Tales From Firozsha Baag*, New Delhi: Rupa Books. 1987.

Mukherjee, Bharati, *Darkness*, New Delhi: Penguin India. 1985.

—. *The Middleman and other Stories*, New Delhi: Prentice Hall of India. 1989.

9

Geographical Dislocations and the Poetics of Exile: Ashis Gupta and Michael Ondaatje

Jasbir Jain

Writers who have moved away from one culture to another are caught between two cultures and are very often engaged either in a process of self-recovery through resort to history and memory or in a process of self-preservation through an act of transformation.[1] Expatriate writers have also been engaged in a permanent act of uprootedness and dislocation through travel and travelogues like Naipaul.[2] Moving outside the nostalgia-protest syndrome, both Ashis Gupta and Michael Ondaatje create a "third space", by moving away both from the culture of their adoption and the culture of their origin and setting their novels – Gupta in *The Toymaker from Wiesbaden* (1993) and Ondaatje in *The English Patient* (1992) – against the backdrop of the Second World War and its aftermath and locating them in Germany and Italy respectively. They project a world which rests on geographical and culture dislocation. Both move away from the implicatory position of involved participation to a postured position of apparent neutrality. Both the novels project multicultural situations in an attempt to minimize polarisation and individual pulls of identity.

The geographical dislocation raises several questions with respect to the poetics of exile, the nature of expatriate writing, the writer's relationship to his culture and his work, the specifics which govern identity construction and the concept of decentring. Is it, at one level, a move out of the expatriate's dilemma of avoiding a schizophrenic split, of being pulled in two contradictory directions, and if so, does it promise release or does it inscribe a new kind of meaning?[3] The creation of this third space does also, at another level, destroy the concept of 'purity' of cultures and brings into being a self-reflexive self and a self-reflexive text. As Homi Bhabha has pointed out in *The Location of Culture*, the creation of a Third Space disrupts "the logics of synchronicity and evolution which traditionally authorize the subject of cultural knowledge" (Bhabha 36). It makes "the structure of meaning and reference an ambivalent process" and "destroys this mirror of representation in which cultural knowledge is customarily revealed as an integrated, open, expanding code" (Bhabha 37).

A sense of place is one of the imperatives of a writer's being, an imperative increasingly being dislocated through extra- territoriality. Nineteenth century writing had privileged the sense of rootedness. Referring to Mark Twain, Henry B. Wonham has pointed out that literary creativity depends on the "unconscious accumulation of local knowledge", and the writer has only one reservoir of unconscious material from which to draw (Wonham 9). Similarly Barry Lopez commenting upon "A Literature of Place" writes:

> I want to talk about geography as a shaping force, not a subject.... A specific and particular setting for human experience and endeavour is, indeed central to the work of many nature writers, I would say a sense of place is also critical to the development of a sense of morality and of human identity. (7)

Natural surroundings, the flow of streams, the direction of winds affect creative imagination as well as the sense of identity. A sense of place, the architectures which the imagination encounters, the openness towards one's surroundings, these impart a sense of belonging and reduce the sense of being isolated. How does the expatriate writer move from one kind of affiliation (culture of his origin) to another kind (culture of his adoption)? When the writer creates a third space, is it because he wants to escape from conflictual situations and self-division, or is it an attempt to negotiate alternate realities? Can this creation of a third space be equated with the use which writers make of fantasy in their narratives, and is it comparable in anyway with the Foucauldian definition of a heterotopia? (Soja 17) Soja draws attention to what he calls the "ambivalent spatiality" of Foucault which was interwoven into "brilliant whirls of historical insight". Space and time are interrelated. History unfolds itself through constructions of space. Heterotopia, Foucault explained, is to be contrasted with utopias. Heterotopia is a countersite like a resting place, a sanatorium, a prison or a theatre, a countersite where "all the other real sites that can be found within a culture are simultaneously represented, contested and inverted" and where a juxtaposition of the otherwise incompatible can take place (Foucault 24-25). If this negotiation within a third space is determinative of identity construction, how does it relate to the writer's native culture? Identity is constructed through multiple specifics – language, myth, history, psychology, gender and race. It is directly connected with the subject's self-image and the unconsciously inherited positionings. The creation of this third space reflects these complexities.

Space provides in itself a dynamics for history. Writers from erstwhile colonized countries and marginalised or inferiorized societies are engaged in a process of reconstructing both national and personal histories with the objectives of analysing and understanding their own past and also as a historical intervention in the master narrative of the imperial races. Space is an important determinant of the kind of relationships which are produced. Power structures indicating exclusion and inclusion are spatial in nature. As Edward Soja has pointed out, "The historical imagination is never completely spaceless and critical. Social historians have written, and continue to write, some of the best geographies of the past" (Soja 14).

Gupta's *The Toymaker from Wiesbaden* (1993) is his second

novel. The first *Dying Traditions* is set in post partition India and takes cognizance both of Pakistan and Bangla Desh with characters travelling to Bangla Desh, United States and Europe. Europeans and Americans also travel to India. Thus these dislocations work in both directions and both exile and attraction work simultaneously. While some characters are exiled, or ousted, or choose self-exile to ignominy, others seek affiliation with alien cultures and are reluctant to return. In *The Toymaker* however the spatial structure is constructed differently. The movement is not to and fro in both directions, instead it is Hans Schroeder who moves first to Siberia as a Russian prisoner, and later, after a stay in Germany, migrates to America. There are two journeys and both of these take Hans to limited enclosed worlds, prisons or prison-like, loveless and airless. *The Toymaker* opens with conjunctions of past and present. Memories float from one to the other. The present is represented by the window protected by barbed wire, the sky dark and featureless (1) and the past by memories of a mice-free world of open spaces and hearsay memories of people scavenging for food (2). Hans's childhood memories are of Wiesbaden as a place seemingly full of magic and unreal happiness. The narrative framing which takes place right at the beginning is a contrast between a world of faith and one bereft of faith. God, if he is not dead, is a distant presence, no longer reachable.

It is within this framing that the narrative plunges straight into a trial for a double murder. Hans Schroeder is charged with the murder of his wife Eva and his daughter Katarina. The dominant image is of a closed space and of unknown terror. The conscious or unconscious intertextuality goes back to Orwell's *Nineteen Eighty Four.*[4] The voice of God and the presence of mice are juxtaposed:

> I've heard the voice of God from time to time. The last time I heard him the voice sounded somewhat faint, like a call from a far away place. I thought about it for a long time, until the mice took over. Now they run in and out of the corners of my mind. Yes, mice have been very much on my mind the last few days. I hate

mice. They're sly, small, crafty, you never win against mice (1)

The first person narration is an entry into the prisoner's consciousness, and alternates with the third person world describing the trial – the long legal advice to the jury, the passages of argument and defense, the prosecution's charges, the medical evidence of emotional instability, the judgement that while one murder is first degree murder, the second a second degree committed in a moment of madness. The inconsistent verdict recognises a split personality which within minutes has moved from sanity to insanity. The alternating narrative voices are worked out quite meticulously. Hans is the narrator of almost every alternate chapter – one, three, five, seven, nine, eleven, thirteen, fifteen and in some measure seventeen and eighteen. The intervening voices are of the narrator, the neutral voice of legal advice, the Prosecution lawyer Concannon's presentation of the case, the opinions of two psychoanalysts Dr. Woodward, and Dr. Mezer, the defense lawyer Piscitelli's argument, a flashback of Hans's courtship of Eva, and letters to Peggy Constanza.

Woven into this narrative are several other narratives – Hans's childhood memories, his life in the army, and his prison term in Siberia where he has witnessed extreme brutality. This prison term is variously described as a period of three years (29), six years (63) and seven years (42) positing an unreliable narrative consciousness which indicates the nature of shifting reality as Rushdie in his essay " 'Errata': Unreliable Narration in *Midnight's Children*" has pointed out. Unreliable narration can be caused by interested parties as also by the unreliability of memory. In *Midnight's Children*, Saleem is an interested narrator as also (Rushdie 23-24). Similarly the accounts in *The Toymaker* are provided by the two counsels. Mr. Concannon mentions the period of Hans's imprisonment as one of three years from 1944 to 1947 (29), while Robert Piscitelli mentions it as a period of six years (62) which would cover the entire period of the Second World War. Hans's own account refers to the period as seven years (42-43). This period in the prison influences the entire course of his future life.

Hans is unable to resume the earlier pattern of life after his return to Germany. The past overshadows everything. The national agenda of purity of blood, the persecution of the Jews, the helplessness experienced in the concentration camp and the witnessing of Tulla's gangrape affect the future course of his life. There is a conflict between his internal being and the external reality, and there is also the humiliation he experiences as member of a defeated nation, when German girls have American lovers (39, 56). The world of Hans's childhood is now totally distanced. Wiesbaden had been a magic place with memories of the past, the Romans who had been there, the baths which people visited in search of lost youth, the Rhine maidens, the opera house which introduced him to the world of passion. Wagner's music opens out a world of infinite possibilities, "I quickly realised I could be anyone I wished inside the walls of the opera house" (4). Faith and music are in some mysterious way connected for him. Later, on his return from Siberia, and during his courtship of Eva, he never visited the opera. It was a world which excluded him, not merely because they were poor but because he had lost god (76).

Hans is twice removed from Germany, once because of the war, and the second time through emigration. His return from Siberia does not really fully rehabilitate him. The seven years had been without any contact with his family and friends. Slowly and gradually he tries to put the pieces of his life together. There is an abnormal concentration in the concept of 'self', his surroundings temporarily fall into insignificance. The destruction around him is symbolic of his own emptiness. Hans as he narrates the experience of this homecoming recounts, "I circled aimlessly through the centre of the city. The life on the streets was utterly new to me, and yet I paid no attention to it. I was looking for the past, my own and that of my fellow Germans" (38). Wiesbaden is an escape route from war-torn Munich, from self-pity and hatred, just as the toymaking is a continuation of his humanity. He had first made toys for

Tulla's child, then in Wiesbaden for the shop where he works, and still later for Peggy's son. Toymaking symbolises for him an identity and is expressive of creativity (37). It offers him a haven from the onslaughts of the outer world, "The toys that I shaped out of wood, the figures I moulded out of clay, all these were pleasurable experiences by themselves. More importantly, they kept me close to children and made me feel like a child" (54).

Hans's second dislocation is set in motion by his wife's betrayal. It is the beginning of a second withdrawal and the collapse of his identity when he submits to the possibility of his daughter being "just like any other American kid" (58). Hans Schroeder's efforts to resume a normal life are interrupted when his wife is depressed and attempts suicide (64). It is at this point that the claims made on him get him down, that he murders his wife Eva and daughter Katarina. Having spent time in the concentration camp, and having witnessed the helplessness of Tulla, he kills Katarina as he himself admits, because "She was a prisoner of her mortal self and I wanted to set her free. I wanted to preserve her innocence for all times, like the Elizabethan from my very first encounter with the opera.... It was my way of returning to my God" (135).

One recurring reference is to Wagner (76) and his operas *Tannhauser* and *Siegfried* (4, 23, 136), to the stories of Brunnhilde who is laid to sleep by Wotan and surrounded by a ring of fire. It is Siegfried, the son of Siegmond and Sieglinde, who obtains the magic ring and passes through the flames to awaken Brunnhilde (123). When he first sees Peggy Constanza, Hans feels it was like Brunnhilde's awakening. There was "music in the air" as he sensed the "unusual beauty of the oval face and the smooth, browned complexion" (123). The references to the Valkyries include references to the mythic hall of Odin where the heroes who have died bravely are received (76, 135).

The act of killing Katarina is a way of cleansing, it is the supreme sacrifice he can offer to his God and his fatherland. In Katarina he sees Tulla reflected. First he had found Tulla in

Peggy. Peggy had brought music to his life, just like Tulla and brought him close to a child's world, "It made me alive once again, made me feel complete. Like Tulla she lost her child. like Tulla she lost her mind" (135). He is aware of Tulla's presence in Katarina as well. He would have liked to name her Tulla, only Eva wouldn't hear of it. Hans's world of the unconscious is a world where dreams and nightmares merge into each other. It is the erosion of his self-image and the loss of his identity (133) which renders him a victim. He feels humiliated, as if he had sold himself by coming to America (95), it seems to him to be the betrayal of his fatherland (77). He would even crawl to Germany (75) to salve his conscience.

To begin with, Ashis Gupta is working out a strategy of distancing himself from any involvement in the historical process. Hans is a German, and the narrative is based on a true life account offered to the writer by a lawyer friend. The exploration of Hans's psychological and historical world is conducted through focusing on it through multiple points of view. But underneath this concern, the concern is with the manner in which nations are constructed (the idea of racial purity), the internalization of the humiliation of defeat, the loss of identity, the conflict which accompanies dislocation, the constant intervention of the past into the present, the denial of freedom and the constraints on the self. Hans's need for Harry is a need for the 'other', is a need to seek verifiability in a world where almost everything is unverifiable. A story, Hans elaborates at one point, is like a toy, much "like the wooden toy I used to make. You whittle away at the wood with a knife, and little by little a face, a figure begins to show. Meanwhile, on the floor below lies a scattered pile of wood shavings and pieces of wood. Are they not part of the toy?" (118). Similarly the gaps in the narrative, the irreconciliability of the different versions, the hallucinatory memories of Hans's himself are part of the narrative which is about enclosures – the box car, the nine by nine space, the barbed window, the prison, the closures of memories, the exclusion from the world of opera and happiness, and about power structures which hold human life to ransom.

Ondaatje's *The English Patient* shared the Booker Prize with Barry Unsworth's *The Sacred Hunger* in 1992, and has recently been made into a much – discussed film. In one of the early reviews Nilufer Bharucha viewed it as a laboured attempt at postmodernist fiction and found it difficult to defend it against the attack of the critics who viewed it as "now you see it, now you don't kind of contemporary fiction" (Bharucha 7). The novel is located in Italy in a villa, Villa San Girolamo, a former nunnery used as a hospital, and now declared unsafe because of the bombing and landmining which has taken place. In it lies an "English" patient whose face has been burnt out of recognition in a plane accident in the Libyan desert during the war. He is being nursed by a twenty-year old Canadian nurse who has had a broken relationship and an abortion and is herself the child of a broken marriage. She has gone through this war with the knowledge that her father is dead, again the victim of a fire accident. Hana has enclosed herself in her passivity and the placing of this man and woman in this ruined villa is an act of willed seclusion. Both are in a kind of hibernation. But their seclusion cannot continue for long. It is interrupted first by the arrival of Caraviggio, her father's Italian friend, a thief and a spy, and then by Kirpal Singh's arrival who is an Indian sapper deputed to clear the mines in the area. With the coming of these two outsiders, disruptive and regenerative forces enter the villa. The patient has long confessional sessions with Caraviggio and as he goes over the past, the account of the expeditions into the Libyan desert are also accounts of a geographical location subject to shifts and obliteration by the sandstorms. The patient's account of his love relationship with Katharine also uncovers his identity. He is the Hungarian spy, Almásy. Similarly Kirpal Singh's full-bodied presence in this world of mutilated men awakens desire in Hana. Both the narratives work in opposite directions. While the English patient's case states that identities cannot be shed or camouflaged, and the past cannot be discarded, the Hana-Kirpal relationship pretends, for a while, that they can be.

Enclosed in the villa, temporarily they concede that the racial or political pulls are irrelevant.

There are several sub narratives within these two main narratives. Caraviggio has a past of his own, there is an implicit involvement in politics and spying. The English patient has also been a double agent. There is Kirpal's training period in England which brings in the colonial-imperial relationship. They are all of a nomadic kind who have traversed different distances. It is only now that they are at a stillpoint, either analysing and evaluating the past, or hiding it and hiding from it.

The narrative moves outwards in various directions. There are in all ten sections of the novel. The first "The Villa" is the central setting, in the second both Caraviggio and the sapper arrive, the third develops the relationship between Hana and the sapper, the fourth is concerned with the expeditions into the desert, the fifth is about Katharine, the sixth "A Buried Plane" is the patient's journey into the past, the buried city, the search for the oasis Zerzura, the interconnection with Kipling's Kim. The seventh "In Situ", meaning back to the original position, is about Kirpal Singh's training period in England with Lord Suffolk and Miss Morden, where Kip's fears of racial discrimination are belied and he wins a place of equality through his own intelligence and merit. The eighth section is titled "The Holy Forest", and is about the Kip-Hana relationship, and the interconnections between Lahore, London and Toronto. The ninth section "Cave of Swimmers" return to the Katharine-Almásy relationship and the last section "August" is the end of the war and its aftermath, the return of hostilities and national pulls. Kip is unable to continue in this idyllic isolation. The atomic explosions of Hiroshima and Nagasaki, he believes, happened only because Japan was an Asian country (286). Racial differences and ideological hostilities cannot be overcome so simply.

Fire is a universal symbol of destruction and violence and of cleansing of all violence. The Clifton-Katharine suicide pact ends in a plane crash, Almásy is burnt in a plane explosion,

Hana's father dies in a fire accident, Lord Suffolk dies while defusing a bomb, while Kip saves Caraviggio by defusing a bomb. He is engaged in clearing the area of the mines but realizes the irrelevance of the task he has undertaken when the enormity of the destruction in Japan stares him in the face.

Of the four people in the villa, three are social or political outcasts, or marginalised people, Hana is a self exile. This grouping functions simultaneously in two ways, centrifugally through pushing acceptance, merger, truth away and centripetally in bringing people together across ideological and racial differences. The English are dealt with only in oblique ways. None of the four people in the villa is English. The English are however there in the background and determine the grouping as well as the dispersal. James Clifton is English whose identity gets lost and merged in Almásy's and whose wife is loved by the Hungarian. Lord Suffolk is English and he attempts to rise above the imperial power – structure by transcending racial discrimination. Miss Morden is able to provide Kip with a sense of comfort and belonging. There are other English connections. The whole question of the civilizing mission is taken up and Kipling's *Kim* is interwoven into the text through repeated references. Hana reads passages from *Kim* to the English patient (93) who comments on the way Kipling should be read (94). When Hana observes Kip in the English patient's company, "it seemed to her a reversal of Kim. The young student was now Indian, the wise old teacher was English" (111). Kim resurfaces again when the English patient rejects all books in favour of Herodotus' *The Histories* (118). On one occasion Caraviggio and Almásy pour over the map in *Kim* "a map with a dotted line for the path the boy and the Holy one" had taken.

The English patient's room becomes a central place for people to relate to and interact with each other. There is a spirit of bonhomie between Kip and Almásy as they share a can of condensed milk. Almásy expresses the view that both he and Kip are international bastards "born in one place and choosing to live elsewhere" (176). On another occasion while describing his accident in the desert he again uses the term, when they hauled him up as "just another possible second-rate spy. Just another international bastard" (251). The implications of this term are ambivalent. If on the one hand there is a crossing of barriers, there is on the other hand a feeling of being anchorless, disowned and rejected. There is also a comment on the construction of identity and nations and on their relevance or otherwise. There are occasions when people are removed from the claims of civilization and placed in state of crisis, or seclusion and during these periods one is at one's most natural. Describing the expeditions in the desert, Almásy comments:

> There were rivers of desert tribes, the most beautiful humans I've met in my life. We were German, English, Hungarian, African – all of us insignificant to them. Gradually we become nationals. I came to hate nations. We are deformed by nation states (138).

If this is to be taken seriously, it is a comment on hegemonic imperial structures. Kip's background substantiates this comment. Nationalities can be ignored when there is a felt need for the Other, or for the skills the Other has, but in all else they are reflected. The Kip-Hana relationship cannot follow its natural course because of the impossibility of a long term seclusion. While Kip is interested in the clues to Hana's nature, she wants him to know her only in the present. Each is wary of the other's past. She is unable to find any key to him, "Everywhere she touches braille doorways" but "He has mapped her sadness more than any other. Just as she knows the strange path of love he has for his dangerous brother" (270).

Kip's whole being is determined by his background. He is tentative in his relationships with people as he comes from an invisible race. At every step he carries his race with him and has to wait for acceptance before he proceeds. His brother on the other hand is more of a rebel, refusing to accept the authority of the English. While his brother rebelled publicly, Kip had worked out silent strategies of becoming invisible. But when Hiroshima happens, Kip has to discard this invisibility:

> When he closes his eyes he sees fire, people leaping into rivers into reservoirs to avoid flame or heat that within seconds burns everything, whatever they hold, their own skin and hair, even the water they leap into. The brilliant bomb carried over the sea in a plane, passing the moon in the east, towards the Green archipelago. And released. (286-87)

Kip can no longer continue to be in Italy. He leaves the other three in search of some semblance of peace. Hana too feels that Europe is too much for her and wants to go back to Canada (296) and thus they go their separate ways to lead their own lives.

Space is used in a variety of ways in the novel. First there are the enclosures – the English patient's room, Kip's tent and Kip's brother's prison, and the cave in which Katharine seeks shelter. As contrasted with this are the vast stretches of sand in the Libyan desert. Landscape and cityscapes are also pronounced. Lahore, the land of five rivers, London, Toronto, these are described in detail. But there are dislocations of space, specially when the process of historicizing takes over. This is done through Herodotus' history and his records of the journeys to Egypt (see the several references 96, 133, 142, 237, 240) and through Almásy's account. This is also done through intertextuality. There are references to *The Last of the Mohicans*, to *Kim* and to *The Charterhouse of Parma*. This is also done through Biblical references which are interwoven throughout but are dominant specially in the final section as the four characters are now in the process of dispersal and disposal. *The English Patient* offers no easy solutions. Nations and cultures demand their own and the past refuses to be obliterated.

There is in both *The Toymaker from Wiesbaden* and *The English Patient* the creation of a European world of memory through references to art, to music – Wagner, Mozart and Verdi – to European history, to its flora and fauna, to city landmarks. How does the creation of this world relate to the writer's relationship with his material and what does it say about literary imagination?

In both the novels, the writer's identity and cultural roots do not surface directly; the adult entry of the literary imagination into the cultural world of Europe is remarkably authentic. Is it then expressive of a need to transcend the limits of culture and relocate human identity within existential dimensions of being? Or is it a search for neutral ground as a strategy of distancing oneself, and does this search rest on historicizing narrative?

The Toymaker through a Kafkasque trial and contradictory narrations of the same happening opens out existential questions regarding freedom, identity, sensitivity and desire for truth. These questions while they universalize issues also reflect ontological concerns. Hans's problems project a colonial situation, and the way brutality affects mankind. Ondaatje who at first sight appears even more neutral than Gupta, is even more concerned with questions of identity and cultural pulls. Through the character of Almásy, the identity or lack of it is projected, and through Kip the racial differences which refuse obliteration and reject invisibility and the national pulls which summon him back. The process of historicizing which engages both the writers, Ondaatje more than Gupta, is dominantly western. The Asian references are through Kim and the Indian landscape, not through history.

In this construction of. a third space, these writers are moving away from engagement with their own cultural and historical past – and are also partly rejecting fantasy and personal memory in favour of the process of historicizing the European past. They are not even engaged with the reality of their present world. Instead they move into backgrounds of violence and a culture which is acquired, not born into. Is this a measure of success, a search for a new readership, an escape from the immigrant self, an absorption into a new construct? If it is an absorption into a new construct it would be very different from all evolutionary strategies for the move into history is a move into the past and does not take into account new combinations. As poetics of exile, the strategy is one of projection through proxy.

Notes

1. Writers of the erstwhile colonies whether expatriates or stay-at-home have expressed their anger and dissatisfaction with the suppression of the native self. They have turned to history in an attempt to identify their strengths. This is perceptible in the work of a host of Indian writers like Raja Rao, Bhabani Bhattacharya, Manohar Malgonkar. This trait also characterises the work of several African writers. More recently postcolonial writing has been engaged with history and a reconstruction of the historical self like Nayantara Sahgal's novels of the 80s, Rushdie's work, and Romesh Gunesekhara's *The Reef* and Abdul Rajak Gurnah's *Paradise*. As contrasted with these Bharati Mukherjee's thrust has been on a transformation and metamorphosis as in *Jasmine*.
2. V. S. Naipaul is a classic example of the permanent nomad whose identity now appears to be vested in a condition of homelessness.
3. Writing about a third culture can also be an attempt at opting out of a dilemma. Anita Desai in an essay entitled "The Indian Writer's Problem" admits to having sidestepped the problems writing in English is likely to create, "by not writing the kind of social document that demands the creation of realistic and typical dialogue by writing novels that have been catalogued by critics as psychological, and that purely subjective, I have been left free to employ, simply, the languages of the interior" (*Explorations in Modern Indo-English Fiction* ed. R. K. Dhawan, New Delhi: Bahri Publications, 1982).
4. Winston Smith in George Orwell's *Nineteen Eighty Four* is obsessed by the fear of mice and it is this fear which leads to his

betrayal of Julia. The presence of mice is indicative of filth and poverty, and lack of interest in human survival. Their scurrying away represents a structure on the verge of collapse.

References

Bhabha, Homi K. *The Location of Culture*. London: Routledge, 1994.

Bharucha, Nilufer. "*The English Patient*", *Literature Alive* Vol. 5 No. 3, January 1993.

Desai, Anita. "The Indian Writer's Problems," *Explorations in Modern Indo-English Fiction*. New Delhi: Bahri Publications, 1982.

Foucault, Michel. "Texts/Contexts: Of Other Spaces", *Diacritics*, Spring, 1986.

Gupta, Ashis. *The Toymaker from Wiesbaden*, Surrey: Spantech and Lancer, 1993.

Lopez, Barry. "A Literature of Place", *A Sense of Place: Regional American Literature*. Delhi: USIS. August. 1996.

Ondaatje, Michael. *The English Patient* (1992). Vintage Books, 1993.

Rushdie, Salman. "'Errata': Or, Unreliable Narration in *Midnight's Children*," *Imaginary Homelands*, London: Granta Books, 1991.

Soja, Edward W. *Postmodern Geographies: The Reassertion of Space in Critical Theory*. Jaipur: Rawat Publications. 1997.

10

M.G. Vassanji's *The Book of Secrets*: A Reading in Narrative Strategy

B. Chandrika

Hero as Book

M.G. Vassanji, one of the eminent South Asian writers of Canada, may perhaps be the first modern Canadian novelist to make a book its own hero. All the human characters in the novel are held in secondary importance to the Book of Secrets, they are all seen only in relation to it. Even people who have no apparent connection with "the book" are slowly drawn into its vortex and absorbed. And this wonderful book within the book is not fiction; it does not have religious backing to influence the lives of so many people, it is only a personal diary—a diary from the year 1913 which has reappeared after a long mysterious gap of 75 years in 1988. Where had it been all these 75 years? It is really a mystery to the people of the past as well as the present, but the story has an answer as it unfurls itself, reconstructing his story and history.

The diary was of Alfred Corbin, the white colonial officer sent to East Africa as ADC by the British Government. After the war when he left Africa Corbin found his diary and pen missing and thought he had lost them. But in 1935 quite surprisingly he saw his fountain pen in the hands of police commissioner Barns who had been presented with it by a police clerk in Dar-es-Salam who in turn had bought it from an Indian called Pipa. Consequently Pipa's store in Dar was raided in the hope of retrieving the diary also which he must have stolen along with the pen but the police could not find it. The diary comes up only in 1988 when Feroze, a young man who had bought Pipa's store,found it hidden safely inside a wall. Feroze, the shoe-merchant, passed it on to his retired history teacher, Pius Fernandez, and the story takes off from here.

"You taught history sir, can you write it?" was the question with which Feroze handed the diary to Pius Fernandez. Fernandez, perplexed by the puzzle of the incomplete diary, tries to fill the gaps to evolve a meaningful story out of it. His enthusiasm makes him write to friends in other countries for information regarding the characters, makes him undertake journeys and research—all done with the zest of a detective. He is surprised to see the puzzle-pieces acquiring life, coming up as real characters whom he has known. The book assumes a magic quality of its own and absorbs Fernandez himself into it as a potential character. But even when the reader reaches the last page of the book, it remains as enigmatic as at the beginning: a book full of secrets.

The (Mosaic of the) Story

When Fernandez starts reading Corbin's diary he does not know that the Amin Mansion where he is lodged by Feroze was the property of one of the persons mentioned in the diary—Pipa. Pipa had named this mansion after his second son Amin who was born in his old age after 7 daughters only to die at the age of 10. Pipa's first son was by his first marriage to Mariamu and he was known as Aku, Ali Akbar, Ali Akbar Ali and finally Prince Ali Khan. Already history has caught Fernandez in its mire, but, unware of that, he reads on about Corbin's nostalgia, being the only white man in a land of African natives, his friendship with Jamal, the Mukhi or the spiritual leader of the Shamsi Community, his first meeting with Pipa who was brought to him as a German spy etc. It was then that Mariamu entered Corbin's life; she came to plead on behalf of Pipa to have him released from the police custody. Corbin learned from Jamal that this beautiful native-lady was Pipa's fiance, that she was the step-daughter of Rashid, the Transporter, nicknamed Simba (the lion).

Corbin's curiosity was roused by this beautiful girl who was being secretly followed everywhere by Simba. Once Corbin saved her from the hands of an exorcist who was beating her up and put her up at the Christian mission from where the Mukhi brought her to Corbin as his cook and housekeeper. She was to be there till her marriage to Pipa. Mariamu was fascinated by the mysterious book in which Corbin made entries everyday; her curiosity was roused when he told her that he had written about her too. (Corbin, at that time, was engaged to Anne in London). The growing intimacy between Corbin and Mariamu is hinted at in the entries, especially where she nursed him during his illness. Soon Pipa came from Moshi and the marriage was celebrated, but on the first night itself Pipa found that his wife was not a virgin. Rashid or Simba, the stepfather, guided his anger to Alfred Corbin and swore that he had seen them sleeping together. The community turned against Corbin and he decided to lie low and apply for leave. But before the leave was sanctioned, Britain declared war on Germany. No one could leave the town. The entries in the diary stopped here abruptly with more than four months of empty pages.

From these empty pages, from where the diary ended, begins Fernandez's quest for the truth. Even though the distance of 75 years is between him and the diary, Fernandez feels impelled "to follow the treads, expose them in all their connections and possibilities, weave them together". He contacts his friends in London to get details about Alfred Corbin. He taps all known sources available. He travels to Moshi to have a look at the memoirs that Alfred Corbin had published, *Heart and Soul*, the only copy being available in the Moshi Library. All his efforts and correspondence bring to his life two people, one from the past and one from the future, both of them related to the persona of the diary, thus linking Fernandez himself to the book of secrets. He shifts from his impassioned spectator-role to that of a participant-actor role when Rita turns up from London with a claim on the diary. The beautiful Rita Gulnar, the American Hollywood star, who had once been the student of this history teacher – a student who was more than a student in ways more than one. Her claim to the diary is that she is the daughter-in-law of Pipa; she had married Akbar Ali, Pipa's son by Mariamu. Her arrival takes Fernandez down memory lane and makes him drown in the valley of the years. She is prepared to tell him all she knows about Ali Akbar in return for the diary and the silence of Fernandez. The other person who comes into Fernandez's life is from the future, young Jamali, the grandson of the old Mukhi, who takes Fernandez to visit his 80 year-old father. The old Jamal laments of his fair-skinned brother (son of Pipa) who had been taken back by the father. From Rita and Jamali, Fernandez collects a few more missing pieces of the jigsaw puzzled.

During war-time Pipa was forced by the British to be their spy. The Germans also forced him to work for them and so he worked for both the countries. The British found him out and arrested him. When he was released he found Mariamu violated and dead. Pipa found Corbin's diary and pen hidden among her belongings. He was quite surprised, for he had seen this mysterious book on the garden chair of Corbin on the day he was leaving Dar. Why has Mariamu stolen them? Pipa was sure that the book contained the answer to all his torments; it would reveal to him who the father of Akbar Ali was, what the relationship between Corbin and Mariamu was ! But, unfortunately he could not read.

Pipa soon remarried and went away leaving the child with old Jamal and his wife. When the Mukhi died his wife brought up Akbar Ali in poverty and poor surroundings. Alfred Corbin, who came back as New District Commissioner to Dar-es-Salam offered to educate Mariamu's son, an offer that was rejected by the poor but proud woman. Corbin was transferred to Uganda and he never came back to Africa. Pipa re-claimed his son and took him away to be educated. Young Akbar was surprised to see the consecrated shrine in his father's storeroom where a book, the diary, was worshipped. It was a shrine dedicated to Mariamu. When Akbar Ali learned to write, Pipa made him write the name Mariamu in English and scanned the pages of the diary to see if the letter-pattern matched with any word there. But he thrashed Akbar Ali when the latter tried to read the book.

Akbar Ali grew up to be a dashing young man and a dandy. He found a job at a firm and married the dark daughter of his employer and became rich. Soon he denounced his humble origins and started going round as the glamorous Prince Aly Khan.

Pipa's shop was raided on two days. On the first day they found nothing, on the second, they came again and headed straight for the store-room. At the shrine they found a book – but it was not the diary, it was a Gujarati book. A fire destroyed the storeroom and with the money he got as compensation Pipa moved to another shop and residence and later built Amin Mansion. When little Amin died at the age of 10, Akbar Ali came from London to console his father and then he learned about Mariamu and the enigma surrounding his birth. Ali had meanwhile divorced his first wife and married the beautiful Rita Gulnar who had eloped with him. Soon he found another woman, Rosita, an Argentinian lady who could adopt to his western ways of living. Since neither Rita nor Rosita insisted on divorce, Ali had two wives now and children by both. Ali met Corbin unexpectedly at some party and they took to each other. Without letting Rita know, Ali met him twice or thrice, as Fernandez learns later.

Even with all these strands in his hands Fernandez feels that there are some missing links in the story. For instance, why was Pipa's shop raided? At the second raid why did the police men go to the shrine as if to find some book there? The answers were found when Rita handed him a copy of poems by Robert Gregory, his old colleague, who had left his belongings to Fernandez on his death. Fernandez had not opened them yet.

He does it now and is surprised to find in it letters from Alfred Corbin and Anne Corbin whom Gregory had met during his short span of service in Uganda. Their letters explain the raid and also tell him about the secret meeting between Ali and Corbin.

Even then, two questions are left unanswered. In order to find answers to them, the nature of two relationships have to be clarified: that of Mariamu and Corbin and that of Mariamu and her stepfather. It is where Vassanji does not come to our help.

Shehru's Art

The gunny sack of M.G. Vassanji's first novel of the same name was fondly called Shehru after Shehrezad, the first storyteller. The mystery of the Arabian Nights spreads through the *Book of Secrets* appropriately set in Africa. *No New Land* has started in the Canadian present, journeyed through African past and returned to the present with a futuristic outlook. I had touched upon Vassanji's tri-continental concern in my paper on *No New Land*. In terms of tri-continental concerns the *Book of Secrets* is linked to the earlier novels in a tripodic structure. *Gunny Sack* spanned four generations of Asian experience in East Africa. *No New Land* took us to Canada, the land of the immigrants and *Book of Secrets* takes us back to the Asian Community and East Africa, concentrating on the experience of the whites and the natives. It is a virtual return to the land of stories and story telling and hence the experimental nature of craft in the *Book of Secrets*.

It has a neat structure, the novel falling into two parts, capped with a prologue and closed with an epilogue. The two subdivisions in Part I and three subdivisions in Part II are separated by small intersections. Vassanji employs a variety of strategies and ploys such as first person narration, third person interruptions, entries from diaries, journals, correspondence, excerpts from actual govt orders, appendices, riddles and excerpts from Quran and Shakespeare. He uses Marquezian techniques like magic realism when Mariamu visits Pipa after her death.

The Beginning

> They called it the book of our secrets, Kitabu cha siri zetu. Of its writer they said: He steals our souls and locks them away; it is a magic bottle, this book, full of captured spirits.... Even now it makes protagonist of those who would decide its fate.
>
> Because it has no end, this book,it ingests us and carries us with it and so it grows. (1-2)

The beginning gives the impression of *The Book of Secrets* as metafiction, for it is metafiction that turns on itself. The beginning itself shows the author's acute self-consciousness about the formal constructed nature of the work. As the work proceeds we see that it is more like a modernist fiction that aspires to a unity of vision, a unity constructed from fragments, or shocks, or juxtaposition of differences. The continuity here is a disrupted continuity. It is this search for a unity of vision that makes *The Book of Secrets* different from metafiction, for in metafiction or narcissistic narrative the search is abandoned altogether. Vassanji is careful to pick up every thread as he moves along and he ties them neatly at the end. But he does not give all the answers to the questions that upset the characters. The question that had haunted Pipa all along -- who is the father of Akbar Ali—is left to speculation even at the end. Was it Corbin, the white man, with whom Mariamu had a mysterious emotional relationship? Or was it Simba or Rashid, her stepfather, who had been jealously following her everywhere and who spreads the rumour about Corbin? Or was it Pipa himself? The fair skin of Ali, Corbin's interest in the boy and his offer to educate him, Mariamu's hysterics when she had lived in her house with the stepfather, the later secret meetings between Corbin and Ali in London, the meetings which Ali concealed even from Rita, all these are pointers, signifiers. But what do they signify? Vassanji seems to often deliberately mislead the reader so as to prevent him from arriving at the truth. Another mystery surrounds the murder of Mariamu. Who killed her? The Germans? The British? Or Rashid, the jealous stepfather who had an eye on her, who had been stalking her?. Why is the Shamsi community cautious and hush up the murder? No clue is provided to find the answers. The open-endedness definitely makes *The Book of Secrets* a modern novel rather than a post-modern one, in spite of the metafictional strategy employed at the beginning.

The Middle or the Riddle

Section 2 starts with a Swahili riddle as epigraph: "The two quarrel by day and make up at night". Answer: "The panels of a door".

Here the riddles operate at two levels: the individual and the socio-political. The great riddle is the trickle of blood found on the bed-sheet of Pipa on the wedding night:

> And as he stared at the dark ceiling above him, slow waves of doubt lapped at his unwary brain. The deed was done, twice – come morning he would show the soiled sheet, banner of his triumph – it had been easy had it been too easy? And suddenly a crashing realization destroyed his composure... banner of his triumph or shame? Quickly he sat up. There was blood, but only a trickle". (105)

One is reminded of the story "The Blank Page" by Isak Dinesan about a convent of nuns who supply bridal sheets to the palace, which would be hung blood-spotted, on the balcony of the palace the next morning with the proclamation "We declare her to have been a virgin". The nuns are given a square cut from the wedding sheet of every princess which they would keep in gilt frames. In fact they have a gallery of such frames with the names of respective princesses.

But in the gallery there is one frame with in which the bridal linen is snow-white from corner to corner, a blank page and significantly it has no name inserted on the golden plate. With the image of the sheets, Dinesan had evoked an ideology of female sexuality built on male control. And here Pipa, irritated at the blank sheet throws the riddle at the whole of the community in a sudden fit of rage.

At the socio-political level, the great war is presented as a great riddle composed of many smaller riddles. This is how the war is announced:

> A great cloud of dust moves quietly down the Taveta Road, leaves much destruction behind.
> —A swarm of loudsts?
> —No !
> —Na-ni? What then?
> —It has many legs.
> —Why didn't you say so? Jongoo? Millipedes?
> —Not at all !
> —Comes in peace, goes in peace. (109-110)

The most interesting riddle about war is uttered by a terrified farmer. He had been urinating under a tree. The tree pissed back from its branches. Then suddenly a branch with many leaves jumped down and ran away. No native is able to find an answer for the riddle, till the riddle is brought to Corbin who understands that it must have been a camouflaged German soldier who ran off.

And the section ends with the greatest of all riddles: the murder of Mariamu after violation. The place was full of foreigners: Africans from all over, Indians and Baluchis. It could be any of them. Perhaps she has been killed by the Sufis of Moshi as revenge. Pipa's suspicion does not fall on Rashid the stepfather but Corbin's does. The riddle is not solved just as the earlier riddle of Ali's parentage remains unsolved.

The End

The end of the novel is quite different from its metafictional beginning and its modernistic fragmentary progress. It deceives us by its very realistic appearance. Pius Fernandez has packed all the materials of his research on Corbin's diary and soon Rita's messenger will come to pick it up. Then, Pius Fernandez informs us, he will be going to Canada and USA to have a holiday and come back to Dar to the position of a part-time teacher that Feroze has found for him. He hopes the new job will allow him to take up some new projects he is planning to do. Rita's man arrives for the package and Pius Fernandez stops writing on 12th August 1988. The novel closes on this open-endedness so that another can start from its point of closure.

"Because it has no end, this book", it is stated at the beginning, "it ingests us and carries us with it and so it grows" (2).

Chiaroscuro

It is long way that Vassanji had led his reader from *The Gunny Sack* and *No New Land* to *The Book of Secrets*. *The Gunny Sack* had no experimental craft in it. *No New Land* marks the beginning of the experimental techniques when Vassanji tries out three sets of characters in three backgrounds. But the two novels deal with the immigrant's immediate problem of coming to terms with the new land, the real and the illusory lands colliding in his psychological landscape. The reader brought along these lines finds his author deviating into a new-new land literally in *The Book of Secrets*. Here the book is its own hero; all the human characters are seen only in relation to it and given only secondary importance. Even detached people who have no apparent connection with it are slowly drawn into its vortex and absorbed. "You taught history sir, can you write it?" was the question with which Corbin's diary was passed into Fernandez's hands and Fernandez really re-created history. For, Alfred Corbin, as most of us know, is not a fictional character. He had been the British Governor of Uganda during the last phase of 1940s. Vassanji has, for a change, used real raw-materials from the historical truths, relying mostly on Corbin's personal diary. If *No New Land* is fiction pure, *The Book of Secrets* is fiction, history and fantasy mixed in a scientifically accurate proportion by M.G. Vassanji, the scientist-turned-writer. The book within the book, the author within the author, the 'book' within the 'author': all synchronize into a peculiar chiaroscuro, redrafting the contract between M.G. Vassanji and his reader(s).

References

Vassanji, M.G. *No New Land*. New Delhi: Penguin India, 1992.

—. *The Book of Secrets*. New Delhi: Penguin India 1995.

Chandrika, B. "A Case-Study of M.G. Vassanji's *No New Land*", *Occasional Papers*, III, 1. (1994-95) 21-26.

11

The World of Neil Bissoondath: Ideology in/and Practice

Sonal Baxi

> 3.(1) It is hereby declared to be the policy of the Government of Canada to (a) recognize and promote the understanding that multiculturalism reflects the cultural and racial diversity of Canadian society and acknowledges the freedom of all members of Canadian society to preserve, enhance and share their cultural heritage.
>
> - Canadian Multiculturalism Act

Canada is a multicultural nation. The cultural pluralism of the country is recognized and supported by the Canadian Multiculturalism Act that proposes to promote respect, unity and harmony amongst the diverse groups that compose the "Canadian mosaic". The official policy of multiculturalism is an attempt on part of the Canadian government to curb racial, ethnic and gender discrimination against immigrants and to facilitate the political, economic, cultural and social integration of the immigrant in Canada. But over the years, Canada's policy of multiculturalism has become an issue of contention as the shortcomings of the Multiculturalism Act have increasingly been felt and experienced by the very groups whom the Act supposedly supports. One of the many voices of dissent is that of Neil Bissoondath—a well-established Canadian writer of Indo-Caribbean origin. Bissoondath's publications include two collections of short stories—*Digging Up the Mountains* (1985) and *On the Eve of Uncertain Tomorrows* (1990) and two novels – *A Casual Brutality* (1988) and *The Innocence of Age* (1992). Apart from these creative works, Bissoondath is also known for his non-fictional work – *Selling Illusions: The Cult of Multiculturalism in Canada* (1994)- -that has made the writer a subject of both controversy and criticism.

Since his emigration to Canada in 1973, Bissoondath has strongly resisted the hyphenated identity of an immigrant that would label him as an East Indian Trinidadian Canadian living in Quebec. He insists on being called a "Canadian writer" because he believes that the effect of such hyphenated phrases "is not to define the word 'Canadian' but to mark a distance from it, the hyphen that links them a sign of an acceptable marginalization" (*Selling Illusions* 118). In his controversial book *Selling Illusions*, Bissoondath explores the gap between multiculturalism as an ideology that aims to encourage tolerance and acceptance between the various ethnic groups in Canada and the reality of multiculturalism as fostering racism, marginalization and "ghettoization". Bissoondath strongly disapproves of the government funding of multicultural festivals for, in his view, the preservation of one's tradition is the responsibility of the individual and the family. He is resolutely against the public display of cultural heritage at Canada's "Caravan" which he has described in *Selling Illusions* as a "Canadian- mosaic version of the Jungle Cruise at Walt Disney World in Florida" (82). The Multiculturalism Act, points Bissoondath, has not established the limits for the preservation of one's cultural values and traditional practices, an omission that has given rise to demands for female circumcision, sex selection and racial segregation of schools. Bissoondath does not deny that a knowledge of one's roots is essential for an autonomous sense of selfhood. At the same time he is of the firm opinion that one must adapt to the changes brought by immigration for "Immigration is essentially about renewal" (*Selling Illusions* 111). My attempt in this paper is to examine the works of Bissoondath from his own theoretical position on multiculturalism and the related issues of colonialism, ethnicity and racism. Exile, alienation, identity and memory are the recurrent themes in the works of Bissoondath. This paper proposes to study how his personal ideologies have influenced Bissoondath's creative handling of these issues.

Bissoondath's creative work revolves around the world of dislocated immigrants transplanted to a new geography and culture. The physical distancing from their homelands propels many immigrants to undertake a literary journey back home. "Re- membering" the past is a strategy often employed by immigrant writers to reconstruct, re-define and re-shape their pasts. In an interview published in *The Sunday Times of India*, Rohinton Mistry, when asked why is it that India continues to engage his imagination, remarks: "It's very naive to assume that you leave a place and you go to a new country and you start a new life and it's a new chapter -- it's not. Canada is the middle of the book. At some point you have to write the beginning" (3). As the beginning for Mistry has been India, for Bissoondath it is the Caribbean islands. Bissoondath may deny the hyphenated identity of a Caribbean- Canadian but an exploration of the past remains central to his works. The locale is a significant part of his narratives. For most of his stories the Caribbean islands form the backdrop of the action. In others, the narrative shifts between his host and native countries, i.e., between Canada and the Caribbean.

Most postcolonial writers delve into their national past that has been distorted by the colonial process. In his essay "On National Culture" Frantz Fanon says that "this passionate search for a national culture which existed before the colonial era finds its legitimate reason in the anxiety shared by native intellectuals to shrink away from that Western culture in which they all risk being swamped" (265).

In *Culture and Imperialism*, Edward Said speaks of "the politics of blame" that ex-colonies participate in against their imperial powers (19). But the spatial and temporal distance from his country has equipped Bissoondath with a clarity of vision and a depth of insight to look objectively at the postcolonial state of his native island. Casaquamada—the imaginary setting of *A Casual Brutality*—stands as a microcosm for the whole of Caribbean islands and literally means "house burnt"; signifying the state of nothingness, corruption, unrest, disorder and easy violence into which the island has collapsed. However, it is the island population and not the colonial powers whom Bissoondath holds responsible for this breakdown. In his interview with Aruna Srivastava in *Other Solitudes*: *Canadian Multicultural Fictions*, he says:

> I'm tired of people blaming all of their problems on what the British did, the French did, the Spanish did. That ignores the fact that we've had a generation or two when they weren't there. You've had these very-educated classes from your own country stealing. *They're* the ones who have created the torture, the refugees, and so we have to move beyond that. It's simply not enough to blame colonialism for everything. (319)

Bissoondath is extremely critical of ex-colonies that have failed to cope with their newly acquired independence. His characters are ordinary people caught in the political turmoil of their country that threatens them with oblivion. Thus many of his characters are seen in various stages of transit. The title story of *Digging Up the Mountains* successfully captures the flight of the panic-stricken Hari Beharri who is forced to flee from his island after his close friends die mysteriously and he begins to receive anonymous phonecalls that forebode a similar fate for him. Desperate to feel secure in a disintegrating country, Alistair Ramgoolam in the story "Insecurity" purchases a house in Toronto. Paradoxically, this investment causes him to feel even more insecure as realization dawns on him that Toronto signifies a second dislocation for his family. Ramgoolam has no choice but to emigrate as the island has "degenerat[ed] into a carnival of radicals and madmen" (*Digging Up the Mountains* 70). Bissoondath does not view criticism of his country as a "betrayal" but as a positive step towards change: "the problem with blaming colonialism for everything is that it allows you to reject all responsibility for yourself. What is needed is extremely urgent self-examination, a look at who you are today" (*Other Solitudes* 319).

Bissoondath does not delve into the pre-colonial past for he believes that the Caribbean history has no glorious past to feel proud of. While the present disintegrates to offer any hope for the future, for Bissoondath, the past too, is devoid of any significance, a view shared by his uncle V.S. Naipaul who writes in *The Middle Passage*:

> How can the history of the West Indies futility be written... The history of the island can never be satisfactorily told. Brutality is not the only difficulty. History is built around achievement and creation—and nothing was created in the West Indies. (29)

Likewise, a character in one of Bissoondath's short stories describes Caribbean history as one that "doesn't lead anywhere. It's just a big, black hole" (*Digging Up the Mountains* 97). Bissoondath's extremely cynical view of the Caribbean expresses his own personal and intense dislike of his native country that acts as a justification for moving to places that offer better opportunities. Ironically, Bissoondath's protagonists lead a bleak life in Canada.

In *The Invention of Canada: Literary Text and the Immigrant Imaginary*, Arnold Harrichand Itwaru writes:

> The immigrant writer is not merely the author who speaks about the immigrant experience, but one who has lived it, one whose response is an irruption of words, images, metaphors, one who is familiar with some of the inner as well as the outer workings of these particular contexts. (25)

Bissoondath's works show autobiographical traces that lend insight into his own ideologies. It is interesting to study Bissoondath's portrayal of the immigrant experience in view of his own remarks on multiculturalism. The two short stories "Insecurity" and "Security" depict the contrast of Ramgoolam's life before and after immigration respectively. While life on the islands held a political threat, in Canada, Ramgoolam feels personally insecure as he not only becomes alienated from his now "independent" wife and "Canadian" sons but also feels uprooted in a new culture. His desperate need to feel a sense of belonging leads him to follow the traditional practices of Indian culture that he had paid little attention to earlier and which now earns him the following remark from his son: "You always did your *pooja*, Pa, but how come you never get into this incense and beef- banning and this other shit before? How come now, here, of all places?" (*On the Eve of Uncertain Tomorrows* 105).

Bissoondath's characters are hinged on the ledge of "uncertain tomorrows"—a tomorrow that often fails to meet the hopes that they carry in their hearts. The story "On the Eve of Uncertain Tomorrows" presents the anguish and despair of Amin, a political refugee who awaits death in his native country after he is refused immigrant status in Canada. Born of a writer who is against the notion of racial and ethnic purity, Bissoondath's fictional characters almost never form their own indigenous communities in their adopted countries and are shown to live desperately lonely lives.

Bissoondath has criticized writer M.G. Vassanji's description of the Shamsi community in *No New Land* as being "so tight, so self-contained, so alienated from the mainstream..." (*Selling Illusions* 110). Bissoondath believes that acculturation can lead to a "multicultural" identity but his fiction shows the strong hold that the past has on his characters. Raj Ramsingh, the protagonist of his first full-length novel, *A Casual Brutality*, is a representative case in point. Raj echoes the author's own sentiments. He leaves for Canada to study medicine because, like Bissoondath, he believes that his country offers little scope for his ambitious aspirations. As Raj says "Small places, places of limited scope, of brutal past, hesitant present and uncertain future, offer but scanty possibility, offer at best a life proscribed" (*A Casual Brutality* 123).

The character of Raj portrays various contradictions. On the one hand he despises the customs and ceremonies of his culture. He detests "being obliged to kiss remote aunts and vague uncles, strangers whom I neither knew as people nor cared for as relatives, but whose cheeks demanded an affectation of affection" (*A Casual Brutality* 69). Despite this Raj is deeply attached to his relations which brings him back home to allow his son Rohan to grow up knowing his roots. Reflecting on his return Raj realizes that "these people whom I didn't particularly like or admire but to whom I felt myself bound — these people too, had played a role" (*A Casual Brutality* 185). On his arrival at the Casaquamadan airport, he is inhibited by his wife's presence in embracing his grandmother: "I knew, then, that were it not for Jan and Rohan, a part of me would be a child once more, revelling in the snug comfort of the familiar" (*A Casual Brutality* 293). Raj is deeply attached to his family though he refuses to accept this truth. He keeps maps of Casaquamada as a memory of his homeland. The strength of his roots is revealed by the following statement: "I am, by birth, Casaquamadan: by necessity disguised as choice, Canadian" (*A Casual Brutality* 30).

Bissoondath believes that integration with a new culture can bridge the gaps at the heart of multiculturalism. But Raj, who is so eager to shed his roots, leads an anonymous existence in Canada. Raj shares Bissoondath's resistance to ethnicity and avoids any identification with Caribbeans in Toronto. He refuses to even meet their eyes on the streets for in their search for "contact and comfort in a brotherhood of skin and race", he sees "a defensive racism, the threat of mental ghetto" (*A Casual Brutality* 200). Raj believes that he "had not come to Toronto to find Casaquamada, or to play the role of ethnic, deracinated and costumed..." (*A Causal Brutality* 192).

Raj is certain that denying his roots and erasing his memories will facilitate belonging to Canada. He makes conscious and deliberate efforts to prevent being engulfed by longing and nostalgia for as he says: "Today and tomorrow were too important for me; dwelling on yesterday could but hinder" (*A Casual Brutality* 143). He prefers to live without any human bonds rather than to cling to his past that could hinder his adaptation to the new land. Even at the Riviera, the nightclub that he frequently visits, Raj prefers the dark corners, avoiding as he says "its openness that was like exposure" (*A Causal Brutality* 240). However, a solitary existence of "anonymity" does not lead Raj to become a Canadian. He isolates himself, refusing to mix with Indians and Canadians alike. His denial of the past further alienates him from the present.

Memories of the past haunt many of Bissoondath's fictional characters. For Bissoondath, the past becomes a "cage" that entraps immigrants and prevents them from breaking away from it which he believes is necessary to be in the flow of the present. His short story "The Cage" portrays the struggle of a Japanese girl against tradition. Michi leaves Japan for Toronto in order to escape the oppressive tradition at home that restricts her growth both as an individual and as a woman. In spite of the freedom that Toronto offers her, Michi returns to a life dictated by her father because though Canada provides her independence, it lacks in foundation. The metaphor of the cage stands for tradition from which one can never escape because "the corollary of tradition's pride is tradition's guilt" (*Digging Up the Mountains* 67).

Nostalgia for one's homeland often problematizes the identity of an immigrant. The pull of the past disorients the immigrant to relocate himself in his adopted culture. Bissoondath has been severely criticized for his objection to a policy that lends voice and space to Canada's "visible minorities". Yet he favours neither the American "melting pot" nor the Canadian "multicultural mosaic":

> The American system likes to pretend that it is possible for individuals to shrug off their past, to pretend that it does not exist, and assume a new identity. Whereas the Canadian one says that it is possible to freeze the past and maintain it as it used to exist, while the country one left, by the way, continues to evolve. The melting pot and the mosaic — they're equally false. There has to be a middle way. And the first part is to have governments and bureaucrats get out of it ..And so my attitude, simply put, is leave it to the individual. (*Canadian Literature* 131)

Memory forms the core of Bissoondath's narrations. Bissoondath's fiction reveals the bond that he has for his homeland but the existence of which he denies in reality. It seems that writing provides a negotiating space for Bissoondath to contend between his memories of the past that is now at a distance in time and space and the displacement of it in its relocation within the new culture. Refusal to accept the term "immigrant" does not eliminate the fact that Bissoondath's fictional world is built around immigrants. Bissoondath says that his function as a writer is "to tell a good story, to entertain" (*Selling Illusions* 182). Yet, he consistently writes about people who have undergone dislocation from their native countries. To a certain extent, Bissoondath's portrayal of the immigrant experience is limited. He rarely depicts the interaction between the host and native culture. Bissoondath believes that the issue of racism is often "over-exaggerated". Ironically, he altogether abstains from writing about racial discrimination in his works. In *A Casual Brutality*, Raj is once called a "nigger" and is physically threatened but it is a minor incident. Bissoondath also overlooks the fact that it is racial prejudices that often lead immigrants to keep to their own communities. In the story "Dancing", Sheila James, on her arrival in Toronto, is warned by her sister Annie: "You must stick with your own, don't think that any honky ever going to accept you as one of them. If you want friends, they going to have to be West Indian" (*Digging Up the Mountains* 198). This statement expresses not only the prejudices that immigrants hold about the dominant culture but also the discrimination they face. Interestingly, this same story explores the effects of "inverse racism" where Canadians are threatened by immigrants who feel that they are entitled to deny the rights of others as they belong to a minority community.

Bissoondath's fiction does not depict the difficulties that meet immigrants. Vassanji may have created a cultural ghetto in *No New Land*. Nevertheless, he has convincingly portrayed the problems that immigrants undergo in a new land. In contrast, Bissoondath's characters live in a self-imposed exile — they neither give up their past nor accept the present. Bissoondath believes that one must break with the past in order to be in the flow of the present. But his characters neither "integrate" nor "assimilate" with the new culture. His characters have a troubled relationship with their past and are confused about their identities. They are involved in an internal struggle to forget their past. Relocation and acceptance of the past is necessary to adapt to a new culture. As long as they do not accept their roots, Bissoondath's characters are doomed to a lonely and isolated existence.

References

Bissoondath, Neil. *Digging Up the Mountains* (1985), Toronto: Macmillan Paperbacks, 1986.

—. *A Casual Brutality*. New York: Ivy Books, 1988.

—. *On the Eve of Uncertain Tomorrows* (1990). Toronto: Penguin Books, 1991.

—. *The Innocence of Age*. Toronto: Knopf, 1992.

—. *Selling Illusions: The Cult of Multiculturalism in Canada*. Toronto: Penguin Books, 1994.

—. Interview. *Other Solitudes: Canadian Multicultural Fictions*. eds. Linda Hutcheon and Marion Richmond. Toronto: OUP, 1990.

—. "Building on Common Ground". *Canadian Literature* 147 (1995): 127-35.

Fanon, Frantz. "On National Culture". *The Wretched of the Earth*, trans. Constance Farrington. Harmondsworth: Penguin Books, 1967. 168-78. Rpt. in *Literature in the Modern World: Critical Essays and Documents*. Ed. Dennis Walden. New York: OUP, 1990. 265-71.

Itwaru, Arnold Harrichand. *The Invention of Canada: Literary Text and the Immigrant Imaginary*. Toronto: TSAR 1990.

Mistry, Rohinton. "How Memory Lives and Dies". *Newsmakers* (The Sunday Times of India/The Sunday Review). 27 Oct. 1996: 3.

Naipaul, V.S. *The Middle Passage.* Harmondsworth: Penguin, 1969.

Said, Edward. *Culture and Imperialism* (1993). London: Vintage, 1994.

Vassanji, M.G. *No New Land.* Toronto: Mc Clelland & Stewart Inc., 1991.

12

Locating the Exile's Culture: Shyam Selvadurai's *funny boy*

Jameela Begum A.

Locating the site has become a narcissistic preoccupation with the postcolonial writer, especially the postcolonial immigrant writer. Exiled by choice or circumstance, the immigrant finds himself displaced from his roots, his antecedents, and his Centre. He sheds his monolithic national and regional identity and becomes a repository of dualities and multiplicities. His position as the Outsider in the country of his adoption leads him to create a distinct geographical and textual space that is contrary to the colonial discourse. South Asian writers in Canada have often been caught within such an experiential ambience. Writers like M.G. Vassanji, Rohinton Mistry, Arnold Itwaru and Uma Parameswaran have consciously created a mytheme that is rooted in a kaleidoscopic projection of the history and culture of the countries to which they belong. However, looking at their writings from a non-exile's position, I feel that this insistence to root themselves within a geographical space works against them at the discourse level. Their thinking is chained to the paradigms of Western thinking. Caught within a system of binary oppositions that label them as the Outsider and the Other they tend to highlight differences and assume a particularization that negates the universalising principles within Western discourse. Yet, this projection of contrariness and difference basically arise out of a social context in which language becomes power. For the Occidental the Orient had been all that he was not in the negative sense. The Oriental writer now sets himself up in opposition to the Other and tries to centre his experience. He travels on the bandwagon of his heritage but with the White Albatross round his neck, choking his very expressionistic powers. Thus the cultural space he creates is crisscrossed by a series of dissensions and the location of his site becomes a transcription or mimicry rather than a translation or a mimesis. Even though he consciously violates the intellectual paradigms of the Western World his perspective is shadowed by his ambivalent relationship. The literature of the exile thus becomes a highly vibrant and violent expression of the split-self. It is not a mere transference of textual spaces. He creates a counter- discourse that is at once referential (geographical) and differential. The differential principle of discourse wherein propositions and oppositions are exclusive of one another is redrawn in the exile's written word. His mimicry or representation is a private imitation and as such controlled by a subjective centre. His romping is rooted in a nostalgic and remembered experience. Here the private and public histories coalesce and are extensions of one another.

What one finds very interesting about a book like *funny boy* is not just the retelling of a history/culture but the way of telling it. Literature would cease to be literature if it is nothing more than a factual historical survey of a particular period in the history of a nation and people. The discourse, the narrative strategies that Shyam Selvadurai employs, creates a textual space in which fantasies and realities coexist. Contrariness and binary oppositions split the novel asunder yet sustain its multilayered structure.

Published in 1994, Shyam Selvadurai's novel *funny boy* uses a boy protagonist to narrate the seven eventful years in his life and that of his country leading upto the riots of 1983 and his subsequent immigration. Arje Chelvaratnam remarks:

> Those spend-the-days, the remembered innocence of childhood, are now coloured in the hues of the twilight sky. It is a picture made even more sentimental by the loss of all that was associated with them. By all of us having to leave Sri Lanka years later because off communal violence and forge a new home for ourselves in Canada. (5)

Arje Chelvaratnam is set within the world of communal violence and relationship that are structured on convenience rather than love. Radha Aunty and his own mother give their hearts to one and marry another to conform to social rules and racial etiquette. Their heterosexual relationships bereft of love become the context for the homosexual relationship that "the funny boy" Arje has with his school mate Shehen. Arje is an exile even within his home. As the youngest, and fond of playing with girls, his fantasies are feminine dreams and wish fulfillments. The feminine role of the 'bride' he steps into at the beginning of the novel is confirmed in the latter part where he finds himself "a funny boy" "a sissy" and is ashamed. The narrative is thus drawn from the perspective of an "exile" or "outcast."

> I would be caught between the boy's and the girl's world not belonging or wanted in either. (5)

The reminiscence thus becomes that of an "Outsider" and 'Sri Lanka' becomes more than a geographical and metaphorical space. It is a psychological projection of the exile's view of his culture and is undermined by a negative stream of events. Thus when Selvadurai in the first story "Pigs Can't Fly" creates an hierarchical pattern of relationships and roots himself in a generational saga he emphasizes his difference and his position as the outsider.

This psychological alienation of the narrator consequently projects a series of marked differences. He is different from those other than his race. The progression of psychological structuring from the analysis of gender differences to racial differences is smoothly done. As a Tamilian, he identifies his essential difference from the Sinhalese when his favourite aunt Radha forsakes the man she loves because he is a Sinhalese and therefore unacceptable to her family. The loosely strung stories, six in number, continue to structure a series of interlocked differential patterns in terms of human relationships, like those of his mother to Daryl and his father to Jegan's father.

Gender differences and racial differences are worked into a generational saga that basically connotes a continuity. The smooth flow of chronology is disrupted by counter forces:

> I was suddenly brought up short by the photograph of my great-grandfather on the wall. I stared at it for a moment, and then the gravity of the looming crisis sunk in. I shivered involuntarily as I recalled what my father had said about the fights between the Sinhalese and the Tamils in the fifties and how many Tamils had been killed. Was it happening all over again? Would we suffer a similar fate to that of my great grandfather? I turned away from the photograph, not wanting to be reminded of what might await us. (88)

This seeming repetition of historic moment is undercut by the strong oppositional relationships like those of gender and race. The continuity rests in the interlocking of differential patterns. The hierarchical family structure, beginning with the grandparents, continuing into the incidents that characterize his parents' false pride and selfishness and extending to the make believe world of 'bridal games' becomes the context for the exposure of the violence and flux that disrupts social living. History becomes a writing and a rewriting. The closures suggested by the six stories that are strung together as a novel is a projection of this. The stories provide closed moments of initiation and revelation even while it extends itself to reinterpretation in the lights of a relative analysis. Here a revisioning and relocation of culture becomes central. The fiction being constituted here is both a figuration of a recovered realism and a gesture towards the question of how a "history" might come to be written in the present.

Shyam Selvadurai confronts the problematic issue of being

different and similar in terms of heterosexual and homosexual relations as well. Arje Chelvaratnam's homosexual relationship with Shehan is identified as one of instinct whereas his parents' relationship is one of convenience. Shehan, the enigmatic boy, is an outsider like Arje at school and it is ironically through him that Arje discovers his own homosexuality. The repetition of history becomes again a matter of concern here when one recalls Arje's father's relationship with Jegan's father – a relationship which had mixed bloods and sealed a friendship.

The strategic shifting of centres in the six stories from Arje's experiences as a boy of five to that of Radha Aunty, to that of his mother's relationship with Daryl Uncle, to that of his father's relationship with Jegan's father, to that of Arje's relationship with Shehan and finally to that of the confrontation between the Tamils and the Sinhalese that lead to the writer's exile, is to be seen as the exile's journey through a maze of experiences in his search for locating a site that is his. Instability and the constant shifting of centres reinforce Selvadurai's narrative strategy of setting up differential patterns within a historical continuity. The recreation of a past and a culture that is far from monolithic and single dimensional not only at the level of the mytheme but at that of the discourse makes Selvadurai's novel *funny boy* an exercise in mapping not just a geographical space or a monolithic identity but a freeing of the Oriental stereotype.

Caught in a flux of oppositional and contrary forces, Arje Chelvaratnam, the narrator in exile, yokes together a subjective and objective consciousness. At one level while psychological and human relationships highlight the subjective rendering of the tale, the objective narrator in him records the exile's perspective of a culture that he can now see only as one ridden by oppositional and prepositional forces. By virtue of the narrator's exile position as also the writer's exile position, postcolonial immigrant writing depicts a multifaceted and vibrant representation of culture. Their discourse draws its sustenance from a counter discourse. Far from narrowing down culture into frozen entities, differential patterns of representation open up original and unique ways of locating the exile's cultural and textual space.

Reference

Selvadurai, Shyam. *funny boy: A novel in six stories.* Toronto: McClelland & Stewart Inc., 1994.

13

Versions of Subversion: *Running in the Family*

Anisur Rahman

Michael Ondaatje's *Running in the Family*, considered by many a postmodernist text, lends itself to a variety of readings.[1] One may also read it along a different line as a text of subversions – both thematic and formal—and underline its essentially subversive nature by which it acquires its intriguing individuality. This partly biographical and partly autobiographical retrieval of subliminal images draws upon the surrealist mixing of facts and fiction, truth and hearsay, narrative prose and evocative poetry, words and snapshots. These seemingly disparate modes of discourse, balanced together in this text, may be explored and connected consequently to approach its possible meaning and form.

All the constituents of verisimilitude and imagination, word and image, place and displacement, to name a few, seem to form a complex structure in this text. In writing the lives and times of his people, as also his own, Ondaatje depends, to a large extent, on the method of destroying and overthrowing, reconstructing and delimiting the traditional tenets of linearity. He administers a test to himself to find out if his word may endure his world and this world may stand up to negotiate with the word. Ondaatje tries to test the limits of art and its vulnerability in a mode where distortions of images, as in an incurvate mirror, ultimately create a sense of the real.

Versions of subversion in *Running in the Family* may be studied both in terms of the subjects of narration and narratology. The two, subverted in a typical Ondaatjean manner, merge together to create an elusive text bringing shocks of recognition to a curious reader. Ondaatje lays down a part of his strategy in the very first sentence of his "Acknowledgments" which he chooses to subvert at the end of the books "A literary work is a communal act. And this book could not have been imagined, let alone conceived, without the help of many people" (205). A traditional reader approaching this act of "communal" and "imagined" writing, this text of "confused genealogies and rumour" (205), is put into doubt regarding the vital questions of authorship and credence just as he finishes reading the book although he has to his credit Paul Fussell's definition of travel books as "a sub-species of memoirs" claiming "literal validity by constant reference to actuality"[2] (203). His reading strategy is questioned further on the following page of Ondaatje's "Acknowledgments":

> While all these names give an air of authenticity, I must confess that the book is not a history but a portrait or 'gesture'. And if those listed above disapprove of the fictional air I apologize and can only say that in Sri Lanka a well-told lie is worth a thousand facts. (206)

Ondaatje's concern for "portrait" or "gesture" rather than for "actuality" spells out his writerly concern and makes demands upon the traditional reader to alter his conditioned response. The author confronts the problem of making a credible choice in writing while the reader prepares to negotiate with his various modes of discourse: photographs, journal entries, newspaper reports, quotations, commentaries on Ceylon by visitors, brass plaques on church walls etc. While constructing a myth of his people and their land, he is, in reality, aware of constructing a credible lie for lies underline the facts in a subversive order. The search for the plausible would, otherwise, limit the infinite space this text aspires to create. *Running in the Family* makes a promise to thematize a condition of Being out of the abstract and the elusive. It is achieved in the book by defamiliarisation and exaggeration and by charting the map of virile human imagination. Both the acts of writing and reading in this book are, therefore, complicated. "No story is ever told just once" (26), we are told at the beginning of the book which is subverted at the end: "You can only write it once" (201). The long journey from the initial to the final stage which comes after about one hundred seventy five pages, underlines the impossibility of the ultimate in writing, what Linda Hutcheon calls, Ondaatje's "historiographic metafiction" (139). This movement from the position of hope and faith to that of despair and fatigue does not point towards the failure of the word but, in an inverse order, signifies its strength with which it holds the world. This and many other instances of reversal of order, leading ultimately to an order of the new, punctuate the movement of the book from the beginning to the end.

Running in the Family is a complex detour into time, space and text. One wonder if it is an attempt at writing "an absolutist history" with "minimalist insights" (44) as John A. Thieme would have it. It does not really matter if "there is little sense of linear movement in *Running in the Family*—a clear historical pattern fails to emerge" (44). Historical relations are straightened in this book in much the same manner as the textual co-relatives are sought to create a rarefied atmosphere in the text. Putting together a composition of over two hundred pages with forty two seemingly unrelated sections, and disengaging from the fetters of sustained linear narrative is, in fact, Ondaatje's major authorial design. Variations in the treatment of language from pure narrative to evocative poetry and vice-versa emerge as an important aspect of his writing technique. Mixing in a whole the past and the present tenses, the observer and the participant, the lonely and the inhabited places, contribute simultaneously to the organisation of the text. Similarly, cartographic, linguistic and human relations undergo consequential transformation as the text moves from one stage of blurring and sharpening the focus to another.

It draws automatically that the reader does not receive an organised text; he has to re-order the fragments of time, space and text. Ondaatje has evolved his individual mode of writing after his mother's "sense of the dramatic" (168) and his father's "sense of secrecy" (168). These figures acting as "strong influence", to use a Bloom phrase, contribute to his writing of the text. He writes:

> My father loved books and so did my mother, but my father swallowed the heart of books and kept that knowledge and emotion to himself. My mother read her favourite poems out loud, would make us read plays together and acted herself, even running a small dance and theatre school that people still remember in Colombo. Her reading out loud demanded the whole room, and while young her grace and dancing caught everyone's attention. Later it was her voice, her stories with that husky wheezing laugh that almost drowned out the punch lines. She belonged to a type of Ceylonese family whose women would take the reaction from another and blow it up into a tremendously exciting tale, then later use it as an example of someone's strain of character. If anything kept their generation alive it was this recording by exaggeration. (168-69)

It is by following these modes that Ondaatje wishes to retrieve the past images stored in his memory "like frozen opera" (22) and wants to "touch them into words" (22). Ina Ferris makes a subtle point while discounting the use of mimetic theories of art and suggesting that in *Running in the Family* "there is no transcription, only inscription" (76). It is in this context that one may explore continuity and coherence in Ondaatje's writing especially when he refers to such seemingly varied material as the fifth century graffiti poems on the rock face of Sigiriya,[3] the poignant lines from the poetry of Lakadasa Wikkramsinha[4] and the wall writings by students on the campus during the 1971 insurgency.[5] He turns the banal into mythic, the concrete into the abstract and tries to contextualise them all on a broader scale. "I write as a reader,"(240) he told Catherine Bush in an interview. By doing so, he joins the peripheries of reading and writing into one. His effort at writing without a palpable plot or design, abandoning the text and letting it remain unfinished, contribute to the cumulative effect of his subversive writing.

Subversive modes in *Running in the Family* engage the reader's attention from page to page. Ondaatje's wish to locate his place is writ large at the very beginning of the book as one opens it to find a map with all the major points of reference which constitute his areas of myth-making. It is a geographical entity with its characteristic contours. There is a simple way of identifying it in these terms: "Ceylon falls on a map and its outline is the shape of a tear. After the spaces of India and Canada it is so small. A miniature" (147). He wishes for yet another way to help it materialise on a different plane with images which may not be quite concrete or real, as all such images are liable to be false. His quest for the imagined takes him to disown all stereotypes as such:

> On my brother's wall in Toronto are the false maps. Old portraits of Ceylon. The result of sightings, glances from trading vessels, the theories of sextant. The shapes differ so much they seem to be translations—by Ptolemy, Mercator, Francois Valentyn, Mortier, and Heydt—growing from mythic shapes into eventual accuracy. Amoeba, then stout rectangle, and then the island as we know it now, a pendant off the ear of India. Around it, a blue- combed ocean busy with dolphins and seahorse, cherub and compass. Ceylon floats on the Indian Ocean and holds its naive mountains, drawings of cassowary and boar who leap without perspective across imagined 'desertum' and plain. (63)

Ondaatje's concern is not for a geographical space with a new name of Sri Lanka given to it in 1972, but a mythic space, a condition of mind. It has passed through the vicissitudes of history to acquire its new identity. It has been, in the past, the route for invaders and traders, rumoured in Greece, Rome, Arab, and China, the abode of Adam and Eve on their fall from the heavens, the seducer of the Portuguese, the Dutch, and the

English. It has had various identifiers: Serendip, Ratnapidi, Tabrobane, Zeloan, Zeilan, Seyllan, Ceilon, and Ceylon. He underlines its innocent lackings rather ironically in the two epigraphs on the page facing the map. One of them is from Oderic, a Franciscan Friar of the fourteenth century: "I saw in this island fowls as big as our country geese having two heads...and other miraculous things which I will not here write of." (unnumbered p. 9) and the other is from Douglas Amareskera who wrote in *Ceylon Sunday Times* of January 29, 1978: "The Americans were able to put a man on the moon because they knew English. The Sinhalese and Tamils whose knowledge of English was poor, thought that the earth was flat" (unnumbered p. 9). Ondaatje puts his epigraphs to new uses. He subverts them to develop yet another view of the land and the book may be read as an effort at underlining this difference. The two journeys to this place in 1978 and 1980 turns out to be his stark honeymoons. He makes efforts to locate and recognise himself among a host of people and places, memories and records, images and metaphors. There is an underlying irony in his return journeys as he does not come to stay here permanently but goes back to his chosen place of adoption. The very act of planning his "journey back" (22) and searching out "possible routes to Ceylon" (22) in the maps on quiet afternoons highlights the vital pull of his soil which he feels even after a long separation. The journeys undertaken are more emotional than physical and help in composing both the fragments of life and the text.

In the seven sections of the book—"Asian Rumours", "A Fine Romance", "Don't Talk to Me About Matisse", "Eclipse Plummage", "The Prodigal", "What We Think of Married Life" and "The Ceylon Cactus and Succulent Siciety"—subversion take place on various levels. Before the reader enters this strange world verging on fantasy and reality, he is initiated to it in a manner which characteristically entwine the two strains together. A beginning like this prepares the reader to bank upon the author's memories which are akin to "rumours" and swarm, as if, to take over the reader and make him believe an incredibly fabulous narrative of life and art.[7] As the narrative moves on, strange situations and characters appear. The traditional concept of courtship stands reverted as an engagement is meant to be broken too soon followed by another engagement[8] Marriages are not kept up as expected traditionally as fidelity does not stand the lure of romance.[9] Idiosyncrasies rule over normalcy, and loquacity comes after gulping the tongue of a horrid reptile called Thalagoya.[10] Travels through the land present a picture of disorder reflected in the imaginative horizon of the author.[11] The loss of sharing the warmth of understanding lingers in the memory.[12] Ultimately, all historical relations turn eerie, events defy date and alphabets turn into heiroglyphs. Suitably enough, the book ends not with the last evening but with the "Last Morning" (202).

Running in the Family is a surrealist picture gallery. It is concerned with image-making and mediation, inter-textuality and decoding. It is a map of human concern, a son's book for his father written together with brothers, sisters, aunts, and other relatives. The father remains present all through the narrative but occupies greater space as the text approaches its end. It is a way of catching up with the unspent force of a character and his interminable story. His family is traced right from the sixteenth century and in the entire family tree the father appears to be the most lovable wretch. He has passed through stages of life from one of great splendour to complete loss, from ethnic glory and exoticism of the past to the effacement of all magnificence in the present. The book about an irresponsible, subversive and erratic father ends on a note as if he has not been read fully: "And yet he is still one of those books we long to read whose pages remain uncut"(200). This observation comes at the end after Ondaatje has finished writing his life, times, and place. This may create an impression of the failure of the text. It is, in fact, an acknowledgment of the immense potentiality the world holds and that every text is only an attempt at coming to terms with the world, and also that it remains, at best, an unfinished act. The story of an extended family broken into many nuclear families and scattered over many lucrative spots over the globe highlights the status of family in our times and the postcolonial search for,what Rushdie calls, the "imaginary homelands". This loss of centrality emerges as an important aspect of *Running in the Family* and this is adequately expressed in the following passages:

> Before my mother left for England in 1949 she went to a fortune teller who predicted that while she would continue to see each of her children often for the rest of her life, she would never see them all together again. This turned out to be true. Gillian stayed in Ceylon with me, Christopher and Janet went to England. I went to England, Christopher went to Canada, Gillian came to England, Janet went to America, Gillian returned to Ceylon, Janet returned to England, I went to Canada. Magnetic fields would go crazy in the presence of more than three Ondaatjes. And my father. Always separate until he died, away from us. The north pole. (172)

Running in the Family has been approached variously applying modern wisdom with reference to "subjugated knowledges" (Foucault), "inter-textuality" (Foucault), "biographemes" (Barthes), "ex-centric dimension" (Linda Hutcheon), "myth of excess of belonging" (Aijaz Ahmad). It is, however, a book of love and romantic hangover, warmth and large human catholicity which the reader makes out only after he has negotiated with Ondaatje's subversive metelodology of treating life and art.

Notes

1. See, for example, Heble, Ajay. "Rumours of Topography:The Cultural Politics of Michael Ondaatje's *Running in the Family.*" Michael Ondaatje issue. Ed. Karen E. Smythe. Special issue of *Es-*

says on Canadian Writing 53 (1994)sl86-203; Huggan, Graham. "Exoticism and Ethnicity in Michael Ondaatje's *Running in the Family*". *Essays on Canadian Writing* 37 (1995):116-128; Hutcheon, Linda. "*Running in the Family*: The Postmodernist Challenge." *Spider Blues*: *Essays on Michael Ondsatje*. Ed. Sam Solecki. Montreal: Vehicle, 1985. 301-14; Macintyre, Ernest. "Outside of Time: *Running in the Family*." *Spider Blues*: *Essays on Michael Ondaatje*; Siemerling, Winfried. *Discoveries of the Other*: *Alterity in the Works of Leonard Cohen, Bubert Acquin, Michael Ondaatje, and Nicole Brossard*. Toronto; University of Toronto Press, 1994. 137-153; Thieme, John A. "Historical Relations:Modes of Discourse in Michael Ondaatje's *Running in the Family*. *Narrative Strategies in Canadian Literature*. Ed. Coral A. Howells and Lynette Hunter. Milton Keynes. Philadelphia:Open University Press, 1991. 40-48.

2. Paul Fussell writes: "Travel books are a sub-species of memoir in which the autobiographical narratives arise from the speaker's encounter with distant or unfamiliar data, and in which the narrative -- unlike that in a novel or romance—claims literal validity by constant reference to actuality. "*Abroad*: *British Literary Traveling Between the Wars*. Oxford: Oxford University Press, 1980, 203.
3. "In the 5th Century B.C. graffiti poems were scratched onto the rock face of Sigiriya—the rock fortress of a despot king. Short verse to the painted women in the frescoes which spoke of love in all its confusions and brokenness. Poems to mythological women who consumed and overcame mundane lives. The phrases saw breasts as perfect swans; eyes were long and clean as horizons. The anonymous poets returned again and again to the same metaphors. beautiful *false compare*. These were the first folk poems of the country" (84).
4. "Don't talk to me about Matisse... the European style of 1900, the tradition of the studio where the nude woman reclines forever on a sheet of blood Talk to me instead of the culture generally— the murderers were sustained by the beauty robbed of savages; to our remote villages the painters came, and our white-washed mud-huts were splattered with gunfire" (85-86).
5. "When the government rounded up thousand of suspects during the insurgency of 1971, the Vidyalankara campus of the Univer-

sity of Ceylon was turned into a prison camp. The police weeded out the guilty, trying to break their spirit. When the university opened again the returning students found hundreds of poems written on walls, ceilings, and in hidden corners of the campus. Quatrains and free verse about the struggle, tortures, the unbroken spirit, love of friends who had died for the cause. The students went around for days transcribing them into their notebooks before they were covered with whitewash and lye" (84).

6. "For twenty five years he has not lived in this country, though up to the age of eleven he slept in rooms like this...

   "Dawn through a garden. Clarity to leaves, fruit, the dark yellow of the King Coconut. This delicate light is allowed only a brief moment of the day. In ten minutes, the garden will be a blaze of heat, frantic with noise and butterflies.

   "Half a page—and the morning is already ancient" (17).

7. "Once a friend told me that it was only when I was drunk that I seemed to know exactly what I wanted. And so two months later...a trick which seemed only possible when drunk and relaxed – I knew I was already running...I was running to Asia and everything would change. It began with that moment when I was dancing and laughing wildly within the comfort and order of my life. Beside the fridge I tried to communicate some of the fragments I knew about my father, my grandmother. "So how did your grandmother die?" "Natural causes." "What?" "Floods." (22-23).
8. "The Courtship" (31-35).
9. "Flaming Youth" (44-47), "The Babylon Stakes" (48-52), "Tropical Gossip" (53-54), "Aunts" (110-12), "The Passions of Lalla (113-29).
10. "Tongue" (72-75).
11. "The country is cross-hatched with maze-like routes whose only escape is the sea. From a ship or plane you can turn back or look down at the disorder. Villages spill onto streets, the jungle encroaches on village" (147).
12. "Words such as *love, passion, duty*, are so continually used they grow to have no meaning—except as coins or weapons. Hard language softens. I never knew my father felt of these 'things'. My loss was that I never spoke to him as an adult. Was he locked in

the ceremony of being 'a father'? He died before I even thought of such things' (179-80).

References

Bush, Catherine. "Michael Ondaatje: An Interview." *Essays on Canadian Writing*. No. 53, 1994.

Ferris, Ina. "Michael Ondsaatje and the Turn to Narrative." *The Canadian Novel: The Present Tense*. Ed. John Moss. Toronto: NC Press, 1985.

Fussell, Paul. *Abroad: British Literary Traveling Between the Wars*. Oxford: Oxford University Press, 1980.

Hutcheon, Linda. "*Running in the Family*: The Postmodernist Challenge." *Spider Blues: Essays on Michael Ondsaatje*. Ed. Sam Sotecki. Montreals: Vehicule. 1985.

Ondaatje, Michael. *Running in the Family*. London: Picador, 1984.

Thieme, John A. "Historical Relations: Modes of Discourse in Michael Ondaatje's *Running in the Family*." *Narrative Strategies in Canadian Literature*. Ed. Coral A. Howell and Lynette Hunter. Milton Keynes: Open University Press, 1991.

14

Ondaatje's *English Patient*: Ideology and Form

Sudha Rai

Ondaatje's *The English Patient* (1992) evidences many features of a modernist work, adopting an approach to the writing of the novel which questions the realistic conventions of the 19th century European novel, while dealing with the historical "realities" of the Second World War. The novel engages with many of the concerns of modernist writing, one of them being a rethinking of the relationship between language and reality, fiction and reality. David Lodge writes in *Working with Structuralism*:

> One way of defining the art that is peculiar to the modern period -- which I shall call modernist – one way of defining modernist art, and especially modernist literature, is to say that it intuitively accepted or anticipated Saussure's view of the relationship between signs and reality. Modernism turned its back on the traditional idea of art as imitation and substituted the idea of art as an autonomous activity. (5)

The novel further engages with central issues in postmodernist writing such as the radical disruption of narrative structures, and the exploitation of the "double" sign, so as to lead the reader to a self-consciousness about the instability of language itself. Terry Eagleton in *Literary Theory* establishes the fundamental paradigm-shift that took place in postmodernist writing (as well as poststructuralist theory) through Barthes's concept of the "double" sign and its difference from the "representational" sign

> The realist or representational sign, then, is for Barthes essentially unhealthy. It effaces its own status as a sign, in order to foster the illusion that we are perceiving reality without its intervention. The sign as 'reflection, 'expression' or 'representation' denies the productive character of language: it suppresses the fact that we only have a 'world' at all because we have language to signify it, and that what we count as 'real' is bound up with what alterable structures of signification we live within. (136)

Ondaatje's relationship to form—realist, modernist or post-modernist—is undoubtedly marked by ambivalences as Ina Ferris's discussion on his narrative art in *Present Tense* (1985) demonstrates. The basic claim that is made in my argument that follows is that the treatment of non-European races in *The English Patient*, especially, as seen in the representations of the Indian Kip, largely relies on the "representational" sign, despite its location in a modernist and post-modernist ethos. Consequently, Kip's character remains imprisoned within the stereotypes and binary oppositions of Western styles of perceptions, what Edward Said in *Orientalism* (1978), characterises as an ideology of Orientalism.

The English Patient is the narrative of four characters brought together, relentlessly, by the circumstances of the Second World War. They are Almásy, the "English" patient, burnt so badly in a plane fire that his face is barely recognisable as a human face. (The story makes almost certain to the reader, that Almásy has been working as a spy for the Germans). The young, 20 year old Hana who clings to the English patient, caring for him loyally and tenaciously, lives with a deep, inner void, a sorrow brought on by the loss of her father, her lover and her unborn child (whom she has had aborted) in the same war. The third character, Caravaggio, a high class thief (a friend of Hana's father, whom Hana has admired from childhood), now has hands without thumbs; the thumbs were hacked off by the Germans and Caravaggio now combats his pain and humiliation by relying on large doses of morphine. The fourth prominent character, Ranjit Kirpal Singh (nicknamed "Kip" by the British), a Sikh, has been trained as a mine-defusion expert, in England, and serves in the British army. The four characters come together in a villa near Florence, recently used as a war hospital by the Allies but formerly used by the Germans. The Germans have abandoned the villa but not before planting bombs in the villa, in objects in the villa such as the piano, and all round the area surrounding it, making life for the inmates immensely precarious and perilous.

Ondaatje places beside the trauma of war, the trauma of love. Both are connected as they "use" up every "part" of the "body". The explorer Almásy's middle-age obsession with his friend Clifton's wife Katharine, and the affair it results in, concludes in the death of Katharine. What love brings him, against the backdrop of war are wounds, burns and scarring memories, as permanent in their residues as the mutilation of limbs and the agonised deaths of victims of the war.

The English Patient offers a mixture of styles, discourses and text-types ranging from the realistic to the postmodern. Realistic descriptions, and they occur frequently in *The English Patient*, have their moorings in details of place and time and sequence:

> In the side pockets she found pieces of equipment to do with bomb disposal which she didn't wish to touch. Wrapped up in another small piece of cloth was the metal spile she had given him for tapping maple sugar out of a tree in her country. (291)

Such realistic passages are followed at intervals by passages of poetic, symbolic or "mythical" text which, fulfilling modernist principles of art, release new significance. Such significances arise when even a line is strategically interspersed: "A scurry in the ceiling like a mouse "(31). The line plunges us into the recesses of the unconscious, disrupting our complacent reading of the realistic text, which directs us in a linear fashion. Characters reach out to poetic symbols, to replenish the imagination, seeking refuge from the emptiness of social realities. Hana cherishes the symbol of a "white lion" she sees on the battlements from her hospital in Pisa:

> Like some gift from the past that had to be accepted. Yet she accepted it most of all among the things surrounding this hospital. At midnight she would look through the window and know it stood within the curfew blackout and that it would emerge like her into the dawn shift.(40)

Ondaatje signposts the possible links between the lion and the English Patient: "A white lion. It was sometimes after this that she had come across the English Patient" (41).

The English Patient builds up a modernist texture of great richness by combining the precision of factual and technical registers with the complex allusiveness of mythical story contained in Herodotus' *Histories*. An extract from poetry, the minutes of the meeting of the Geographical Society which met in London in the 1940s, and the scientific text-type which describes the parts of a bomb, bring together the conventions of varying texts.

The range extends to large-scale philosophical meditations as when Almásy asks: "Did I tell you my concept of Virgilian man, Kip ? Let me..." (89).

Paintings and statues which hold a compelling attraction for Kip, locales for lovers' union and separation set in the Cave of Swimmers, whose walls are covered by the frescoes of prehistoric art combine "non-verbal", visual textual signals so as to emphasise the modernist recovery of deeper realities than those available in a world destroyed by greed and brutality.

Ondaatje's resource as expatriate Sri Lankan writer, identifying his art with the modernist tradition, brings in the "meeting of cultures" theme, and *The English Patient* brings in the essences of foreign cultures and the shifting cross-perspectives of Indian upon British, British on Indian, Canadian on Sikh etc.

The sacred and the sacrilegious no longer occupy a hierarchy of value. A dog's paw and the smells it carries can be equated through the selection of metaphoric comparisons with a "cathedral":

> It's a Cathedral ! her father had said, so-and-so's a garden, that field of grasses, a walk through cyclamen—a concentration of hints of all the paths the animal had taken during the day. (8)

The concern with national and cultural identity is once again a modernist theme, but what is important is the manner in which Ondaatje employs it at the level of form to set up currents of uncertainties around the narrator and his relationship with the reader, encouraging the reader to interpret and make meaning for herself. The centre of responsibility has shifted from author to reader, a tendency which will be explored much more radically in postmodernist writings.

Another modernist feature found in the *English Patient* is the disruption of time, despite the dates pinpointed at periodic intervals in the narrative for the progress of the geographical explorations into the Gilf Zebir, the love affair between Katharine and Almásy in Cairo, and the final stages of the Second World War in and around Florence.

Psychological time being more valued than chronological time, characters structure time in individual ways according to their experiences, memories, location in loved or loveless states. History often becomes a chain of idiosyncratic images and actions; the personal submerges the social organisation of time.

In *The English Patient* Ondaatje involves his art in certain forms of experimentation which bring him to the brink of postmodernist positions. Three of the strategies which will be analysed here are: (a) the notion of "intertextuality", (b) the radical instability of language and self-consciousness about the uncertain relationship between "language and reality" and (c) the reader as writer of the narrative.

Terry Eagleton in *Literary Theory* makes the point about the notion of "intertextuality" that:

> All literary texts are woven out of other literary texts, not in the conventional sense that they bear the traces of 'influence' but in the more radical sense that every word, phrase or segment is a reworking of other writings which precede or surround the original work. (138)

The English Patient creates a chain of intertextuality (for the reader to investigate) by focusing on the relationship between other texts and the meanings they arouse, through the conscious (the author's) and unconscious (the reader's) juxtapositioning of texts. Almásy carries Herodotus' *Histories* on his explorations; it is his "commonplace book", which he disrupts wilfully:

> He bought pale brown cigarette papers and glued them into sections of the *Histories* that recorded wars that were of no interest to him. (172)

Almásy is also Odysseus, eternal voyager—literary myth intertwines with the presence of historical fact, which is the "reality" of the *Histories*. A web of "intertextuality" is spun by the co-presence of literary works including Kipling's *Kim, The Last of the Mohicans, The Charterhouse of Parma, Anna Karenina* etc. which bring in an infusion of other cultures. Kip is the truncated Kipling, embodying the romantic, fantasy presence of India to Hana.

Kip is Lord Suffolk's pupil as Kim was the Llama's; Hana is woven into a text of paintings already set up for Kip, faces of women which express sadness and Kip's Queen of Sadness, painted frescos and the villa with painted seasons in rooms. Odysseus' "age" overlaps with Almásy's, Katharine ties in with Candaule's wife in *Histories*. Bits of music, Eliot's "Wasteland", belief in fairies, and stories of dogs, are other texts which discharge accumulated meanings and fresh ones. European cultural traditions are commingled with Indian, African and Bedouin, liberating ripples of additional meaning. Multiple texts of wanderers, exiles, saints, lovers, historians and poets, fire and water crowd into the intertextual tunnel, coming out in new forms. Hana's loss of a father, and Kip's loss of a father-figure in Lord

Suffolk are other overlapping texts, which release ironies.

The English Patient is rooted in a linguistics of the narrative text, pursuing the levels of sound, syllable, vocabulary, grammar, image, metaphor, allusion, history (1483 or 1945) and culture, which impinge on the making of sliding significance in the text. Language is intensively and self-consciously analysed, so as to expose the element of choice and artifice in processes of manipulating meaning. There is also evidently, a relishing of such processes by the author. As Caravaggio has perceived:

> Words are tricky things, a friend of his has told him, they're much more tricky than violins. (37)

Examples of the mobility of metaphors and their significances, as also the English Patient's subjectivity inscribed as a prime value into the act of perception, are found in the following extract:

> He glares out, each eye a path, down the long bed at the end of which is Hana. After she has bathed him she breaks the tip off an ampoule and turns to him with the morphine. An effigy. A bed. He rides the boat of morphine. It races in him, imploding time and geography the way maps compress the world onto a two dimensional sheet of paper. (161)

Almásy directs Hana on the "art" of being a "reader" of Kipling: "Your eye is too quick and North American. Think about the speed of his pen. What an appalling, barnacled old first paragraph it is otherwise" (5).

Ondaatje's shift towards post-modernist disruptions of narrative structures is indicated by the increasing reliance on the reader as writer of the text (Eagleton 1983).

Dramatisations of the shift encouraged come through in the part played by Hana, Katharine and Almásy, as writers, recording private associations, feelings and impressions into books thought of as complete, such as the *Histories* or *The Last of the Mohicans*. There is no absolute writer, who has had the last word in the book, or about its meaning:

> And in his commonplace book, his 1890 edition of Herodotus' *Histories*, are other fragments – maps, diary, entries, writings in many languages, paragraphs cut out of other books. (96)

Reflections on ambiguous spaces in texts and between speaker/reader and listener/interpreter as well as possibilities of plural interpretations of encoded meaning emerge in this extract from Almásy's diary entry, which is written into the *Histories*:

> May 1936.
>
> I will read you a poem, Clifton's wife said, in her formal voice, which is how she always seems unless you are very close to her. We were all at the Southern Campsite, within the firelight.
>
> I walked in a desert
> And I cried:
> "Ah, God, take me from this place !"
> A voice said: "It is no desert."
> I cried: "Well, but
> The sand, the heat, the vacant horizon."
> A voice said: "It is no desert."
>
> No one said anything
> She said, that was by Stephen Crane, he never came to the desert.
> He came to the desert, Madox said.

In the poem by Stephen Crane the "I" offers an argument establishing the signs "sand", "heat" and "vacant horizon" as equivalent to the signified "desert"; but "the voice" disputes the significance obtained and contradicts it. Similarly, Katharine and Madóx (another explorer and member of the Geographical Society) question each others assertions about Stephen Crane—the reader of any text inscribes her/his own meaning.

Ondaatje's technique makes clear that it is not his intention to give complete knowledge or certainties of fact and experience. Like the gaps in the stories Hana is reading out to the English Patient (gaps which she finds unimportant and therefore doesn't try to bridge), like the accidental, natural or deliberate blanking out of memory for the English patient, the novelistic technique thrusts upon the reader, the responsibility of filling in the gaps. The gaps are "like sections of a road washed out by storms" (7) making the reader's journey directionless and erratic.

Reading and its privileges, books and their near magical power are frequently pinpointed:

> Books are important for Hana. This was the time in her life that she fell upon books as the only door out of her cell. They became half her world. (7)

The ending of *The English Patient* places before us the author's relegation of his power over the narrative. Hana, as the narrative voice tells us, has a life of her own: "She is a woman I don't know well enough to hold in my wing, if writers have wings, to harbour for the rest of my life." (301) The ending describes a random play of events, and even as the reader tries to connect, the narrative resists a sentimental resolution of the "bond" between Hana and Kip:

> And so Hana moves and her face turns and in a regret she lowers her hair. Her shoulder touches the edge of a cupboard and a glass dislodges. Kirpal's left hand swoops down and catches the dropped fork an inch from the floor and gently passes it into the fingers of his daughter, a wrinkle at the edge of his eyes behind his spectacles. (301-302)

The English Patient, as has been argued so far, is a narrative which positions its preferred approach to the novel's character and function, along largely modernist techniques, while increasingly indicating its drift towards an intensification of these techniques into postmodernist choices in dismantling "realistic" narrative structures. These techniques are extremely effective in liberating Hana as a gendered subject, to cite one example of how subjectivities are "freed" by the rethinking about form. Hana's individuality is released into greater and greater freedom by the fluidity of signs which describe her and her actions, her thoughts and fantasies. Whether it is the game of hopscotch Hana plays by herself, the footprints she leaves in the library as she enters, and then intelligently retraces, or the rebirth of the

English patient in her consciousness, Hana is released from patriarchal, societal and ideological bondages: "She is a woman of honour and smartness whose wild love leaves out luck, always taking risks, and there is something in her brow now that only she can recognise in a mirror." (301)

With the non-European subject, in this case the Sikh Ranjit Kirpal Singh, Ondaatje relies upon disproportionate levels of realistic representational portraiture, so that Kip remains caught within the fixed stereotypes and conventions of an Orientalism, packaged from European perspectives. It is the "disproportion" between "fluid signifiers" (used for Hana) and their expanding range of significances, and "fixed signifies" which is of interest and may highlight the problem of choice of form and its implications, both interpretative and ideological.

We notice that Kip's bathing, eating and religious habits are observed and commented on by Hana, Caravaggio and the narrator in ways which "objectify" him as "the other". Kip is always formal, never entering the villa except for specific reasons. He constantly explains his actions and Indianness: "I grew up in India, Uncle. You wash your hands all the time. Before all meals. A habit. I was born in the Punjab." (76) A detailed account of Kip's eating preferences and the tooth powder be brushes his teeth with are provided to us. Caravaggio equates Kip with an "animal":

> There is probably some rare animal, Caravaggio thinks, who eats the same foods that this young soldier eats with his right hand, his fingers carrying it to his mouth. (87)

Kip is represented as "emotional" rather than intellectual, skilled with his hands (which dismantle bombs) rather than his intelligence. Kip we are told "did not yet have a faith in books."

Kip's mentors in England, during his training as a sapper— Lord Suffolk and Miss Morden – are surprised and disappointed when given the choice of an English play to watch, he chooses *Peter Pan*: "He had selected *Peter Pan*, and they, wordless, acquiesced and went with him to a screaming child-full show" (197).

Kip's approach to art and music once again underlines his simple, child-like, instinctive approach to the world around him in England and Europe. Watching the five-foot tall statue of the Virgin Mary from the beach, on the occasion of the Marine Festival of the Virgin Mary, Kip is allowed no freedom of movement, portrayed as occupying the site of religious orthodoxy: "If he could have parted with it, the sapper would have left something there as his gesture. But he had his own faith after all (80). For Hana, Kip is not only India, but Asia:

> She imagines all of Asia through the gestures of this one man. The way he lazily moves, his quiet civilisation. (217)

Kip is sanctioned "duty", but, despite the fervour of his affair with Hana, relegated to the first principles of country and religion and later, wife and family. The forms of representation Ondaatje chooses for Kip, permit him to play no games with his own culturally given identity, unlike Hana, Almásy or Caravaggio.

Kip is a spent force, grown old, unable to bear even "the sun of India" as Ondaatje takes leave of him. Kip remains content with sentimental memories of Hana, experiencing twinges of conflict which can never be carried forward. He is allowed to summarise his own closed options, ineffectual in reaching out to Hana:

> It seems every month or two he witnesses her this way, as if these moments of revelation are a continuation of the letters she wrote to him for a year, getting no reply, until she stopped sending them, turned away by his silence. His character, she supposed. (300)

Kip is fixed as an icon of ageless India, participating in imagined and romanticised ritualistic forms such as celebrating the years of the century in 1945, by lighting oil lamps in snail shells, claiming: "Where I come from, we celebrate the age as well as ourselves" (267).

In its affirmation of the reductive stereotypes of non European races, Ondaatje's *English Patient*, as seen in particular representations of Kip, indicates its preference for occupying unidirectional perceptions and the restrictions on narrative form, the limited play of significances, constituting the orientalist text which express it. Despite its openness to modernist and postmodernist experimentation, the novel, it seems to me, exhibits an ideological contradiction raising necessary questions about the implications of modernist and/or postmodernist choices of form and the contexts in which they are chosen.

References

Eagleton, Terry. *Literary Theory: An Introduction* (1983). Oxford: Blackwell Publishers, 1995.

Lodge, David. *Working with Structuralism: Essays and Reviews on Nineteenth-and Twentieth-Century Literature* (1981), London: Ark Paperbacks, 1986.

Moss, John. Ed. *Present Tense: The Canadian Novel, Volume IV*. Toronto: NC Press Limited, 1985.

Ondaatje, Michael. *The English Patient*, Vintage Books Canada Edition, 1993.

Said, Edward. *Orientalism* (1978) Harmondsworth: Penguin, 1995.

15

The Fourth Dimension: Treatment of Time in Ashis Gupta's *Dying Traditions*

Veena Singh

Time past and time future
Allow but a little consciousness.
To be conscious is not to be in time
But only in time can the moment in the rose-garden,
Be remembered; involved with past and future.
Only through time time is conquered.

(*Four Quartets* 16)

Time has been a major concern for writers and more so with modern writers. Referring to the important aspects of fictional form J.H. Miller in his article "Three problems of fictional form: First person narration in *David Copperfield* and *Huckleberry Finn*" writes, "Time is constitutive for the novel in a way which makes it different from other forms of literature."(22) He further adds:

> It is much easier to talk about a work of literature as if it were a spatial mosaic than to do justice in critical language to its temporality of literature is time. (23)

Ashis Gupta's *Dying Tradition* is a novel which concerns itself with the various aspects of time. Throughout the narrative the very simple and elementary notion of time – conceptual time, time as is commonly referred – time by the clock is conveyed through words and phrases like, "an hour", "a day", "a month", "four months ago", "each year from February to October", "from eleven to twelve each morning", "rooms brightened by the sun at that hour remained so for hours", "during the October fair", "at last it was time to go, time to take the trip".

The movement of time is also conveyed through the progression of seasons for example reference to Summer, Winter, Fall, Monsoon or a reference to the change in weather. In addition to this the passage of time is expressed through linguistics: "platform now stood blackened"; "Built nine years since"; "Once been a correspondent"; "day to day"; "time to time"; "Panchu has a childhood limp"; "Over a span of time"; "to this day"; "moments later" to quote a few. Depiction of events in sequence is very simple but deliberate fragmentation of time makes the narrative more appealing as experiences, thoughts and emotions proceed a different pace, beyond the arms of the clock. According to Sudhakar Marathe a narrative beginning is a "triple phenomenon" – the narrative's beginning: the author's beginning, the work's beginning, and the reader's beginning (16).

Referring to the author's beginning he says it is the beginning of the book, "as of a new acquaintance", this for the reader "is an initiation" and the reader accepts it as the beginning. Any book at the beginning is a "prospect" but as the narrative progresses and finally ends it turns to "retrospect". Also with each reader it is a fresh "prospective viewing of a retrospect". The narrative of the book could begin with past history "retrospective" narrative or it could be "prophetic" when it is just fictional history. For Marathe the involvement of the reader with a text is of vital importance.

The beginning of *Dying Traditions* indicates and prepares the reader for the multiple levels at which time is going to be treated in the novel. All is over now when the story is narrated by the omniscient author who is also an eyewitness to every event that has occurred. In his words "'I am his occasional messenger, I replied, pointing to Rahul, who assured him that I was a friend and could be trusted'" (65). At the very outset it is mentioned that it was "another morning" which "ended" with a miracle. We are also told, "the house was alive once more" and that perhaps Sambhu Narain's son would never have a family of his own". On the one hand is the narrator's – the pseudo author's — fictive present; the actual time when the narration is carried forward, and on the other hand is the past in which the story is ingrained. The words "alive once more by implication suggest a past as do the words 'he would never have...." suggest the future. This kind of displacement that is possible only in the narrative, is not possible in life nor in any static art like painting. Nevertheless, the forward and the backward movement is very close to life. According to Mendilow:

> The modern novelist holds that we are at any moment the sum of all our moments, the product of all our experiences. Everything we have seen, everybody we have met is part of us. To convey an impression of this permeation, a multiple presentation of times and people and things fused together is needed.(223)

When we think,the past, the present and the future all come together. The past or the present can never be visualized in isolation. On the contrary, the present becomes more meaningful because it is directed or influenced by the past. Likewise in the present lie the seeds of future. Time is embryonic, conferring a multiplicity upon unity, and as T. S. Eliot in "Tradition and the Individual Talent" has observed:

> the difference between the present and the past is that the conscious present is an awareness of the past in a way and to an extent which the past's awareness of itself cannot show.(296)

The past as such is relative. Its significance and meaning shift and exist only vis-á-vis the present. Thus the past is not separate and complete but part of an ever-developing present. In the novel, the realization about the path to salvation and eternity dawns upon Sambhu Narain only after the loss of his son and daughter. In Rahul's case it is the past experience namely, jail break and the consequent escape to America, and disillusionment with Maoism that helps him mature. Ann Swinfen referring to time writes:

> The view from a moving railway carriage is continually changing, but the entire composite view exists both at the beginning and end of the journey, and more closely resembles the view from a high-flying aircraft. If time is considered in this way, the present moment is like the brief glimpse from the train window, but all time, like the whole scene, exists eternally.(46)

Dying Traditions is a story of a family, a story concerning the ups and downs of three generations -- Sambhu Narain, his children and his grand-daughter. It is also the story of the nation, torn apart by violence and a comment on cross-cultural encounters. It therefore takes into account the personal past, the past of the centuries of tradition and the past of the different cultures and international relationships.

The main incidents and happenings of the novel span over a period of about five years. Krishna's incident occurred in 1971, and the change of government in Bengal in March 1968 and that is also the year of Rahul's escape to America after attempted jail break. The references to Sambhu Narain's visit to London in 1939, his moving to Bishnupur in 1959 take the story further back in time. Malini's death in America two years after her graduation stretches the span of time beyond 1971.

The story obviously, as it unfolds, does not follow the linear time sequence. The linear time displacement results in the co-existence of all time. The story begins as near the end and introduces the previous occurrences. The book begins with the ascetic Sambhu Narain's return to have a glimpse of his house and a second disappearance. We are told he returned "one more time to die".(3) The activities of his younger days, the evening when the message of Sanjit's death reached him, are narrated in great detail. Immediately there is a shift both in locale and time. We are introduced to Malini who is going through her diary – a record of her past one year's activities. Sambhu by then is dead. Kripal's memories of the partition and Alice and Vikram's alliance is narrated. There is again a very obvious shift. Roger and Chhotki incident takes the reader to the tea gardens and also indirectly to the colonial past and the Britishers. The narration then shifts to Noor Mohammed and his son Hamid and finally back to Sanjit's funeral, after which Sambhu Narain did not return home. It is here for the first time that the narrator speaks in the first-person, which gives the sense of immediacy and directness and the novel returns through the past to the narrator himself in the present perhaps now at a higher level of comprehension, and thus the fictional time is destroyed by the "I" of the narrator. In fact, direct speech, anywhere in the novel has this effect and suggestion.

The narrative continues in wave-formation. We are told of Rahul in America on a scholarship, back in India, and his escape to America; we are then told of the journey that Vikram with his family and Hamid undertook to Chirribilli by road. Hamid's sad recollections of his lost love and the unhappiness at blind Malini's birth is narrated. Rahul's restlessness in America, his brooding over "thirty years fading to nothing" and the "unbridled violence of his thoughts"(113) is reported. The narrator moves on to Krishna and Vikram reaching Darjeeling where they mentally go back six years and relive their honey-moon days. References to the Bangladesh war, and the insurgence of the refugees is given in detail. The book ends with Krishna's death. A dark figure of a holy man, only recognized by the narrator, is seen kneeling by her dead body commenting upon Time and Eternity. The narration comes full circle. This looping in time gives a sense of the complexity that is life. If the events had been related to each other as chronology it would have been history in the ordinary sense of the word and not only would it have weakened the structure of the novel but also not been able to hold the reader's interest.

The small digressions and stories within the story, for instance the description of Sir Ajoy's ancestral house and his own past, Chhotki-Roger incident, Sambhu Narain's love for the stage, music and western clothes are deviations in time but these stories with a subjective quality are an integral part of the narrative as they comment on the social scenario, quality of life and the dying traditions. Another example of the departure in time are little Susan's stories. After the separation of her parents little Susan concocts a happy family scene. She says "we dropped daddy at the bank then Mummy and I went shopping" (85). This creation of past and future ends up in the disruption of the child's frame of reference and also leads to the fragmentation of the emotional self. Her stories about "a big bad Wolf", "an alligator", "a big bad fox" also point to this.

References to other texts and authors in the course of the narration also disrupt the present, Sambhu Narain sits behind his desk with volumes of Johnson, Boswell, Scott and Dickens piled in front of him a souvenir of his past for "he would gladly give the others away to friends and relatives except for the lingering memory of his father whose books they were" (9). At once Sambhu Narain is in the present (in past) secretly wishing his sons would read these books. Similarly mention of E.M. Forster's *A Passage To India* recalls the age old love-hate relationship between Muslims and Hindus(4). Sharmila sings songs from Tagore, "songs he (Rahul) was beginning to forget" (152).

Every character in the novel makes a nostalgic safari to the past underlining the role of memory. The memories of the partition haunt Kripal, "the laughter as well as the terror" and "his father moaning and the chilling scream" and his brother's "terrified call for help"poison his sleep (37-38). For Alice the moment of her gang rape lies "frozen in her mind" (35). The brutal abuse of the female body (of Krishna) is an ever present pain to Hamid(200). The memory of Saira, Hamid's lost love, also never leaves Hamid. Molly's mind, "kept slipping back to memories of uncle Kerry"(29) as she lay in the hospital. Going back to the past could also be pleasurable as is in the case of Sir Ajoy who, "liked to think of his own childhood as having been exciting, carefree, even wicked" (301). Past memories haunt Rahul who remembers that "there was a time when he wanted to be one with the conquerors of the world" but by contrast his "now" (life in America) appeared "badly ordered" and "teetering over his head". This reference to a definite specific past by Rahul high-lights the meaningless "present" of his life. Past memories could also be a fulcrum and an anchor as for Rahul. He could not forget his hatred for his father's pretentious world but one image kept coming back to him.

> Everytime he looked back over the hump that separated their lives, he was still walking with his hand in his father's... still strained to keep pace with his father's enormous strides (197).

Past is also captured and relived through photographs and slides. John Newton relives his Zambia experience while showing the slides (84-85). The more one wants to escape the past the more one remembers and pictures from the past flash back and forth. As memory cannot be wiped out it does not allow the past to be past. The indelible prints of the past make it impossible to escape the past. Past becomes eternal, however one can only recollect and relive the past but not remake the past.

Like memory, imagination too disrupts time but its scope is wider than memory as imagination can hold the past, the present and also the future. Rahul's memory frames the faces "he remembered, not as they might really be in life or death, but as he cared to remember them. He felt great playing God,..."(288) many a time the pervading atmosphere of America merges gradually into a sense of time change resulting in Rahul dreaming, recollecting the past and introspecting. Rahul realises:

> The quest for artistic fulfillment and worldly satisfaction can, and must, be yoked together... Daedalus must be resurrected in Harvard square. This land is one of dreamers trapped by their dreams,... it's not what you think you are that matters, it's where you end up that really counts... But do I have the time to watch the birds come and go...? As I had imagined I would.(117)

Time is also a mental phenomenon, static or moving on, depending on the state of the nerves of an individual. Rahul's failed affair with Ginny makes him "slow down" and also realize that the strings of life are held by the hands of time. He wonders "Must he learn to measure his life by the hour...?(112) When he looks at the clock he finds "the clock stood still at twenty after eight. It suddenly occurred to Rahul that he had willed himself to an eternity of twenty after eight". (113) Similarly after Krishna's return from the nursing home, the house "drifts into a curious state of apathy" and "the days became interminably long for every one".(227)

In the novel in addition to time in terms of dates, memories, imagination, psychological and the perceptual time there is historical time which is an important framing strategy. The sense of the past, as Trilling in his essay of that title has pointed out:

> we would perhaps be stronger if we believed that now contained all things... Without the sense of the past we might be more certain, less weighted down and apprehensive. We might also be less generous, and certainly we would be less aware. In any case, we have the sense of the past and must live with it, and by it.(261)

For Trilling, historical sense is also the critical faculty which "is to be understood as the critical sense, as the sense which life uses to test itself."(270) The title *Dying Traditions* itself is a pointer to time. Traditions are rooted in the past, inherited and passed on by generations through ages and a legacy for posterity.

The major events in the novel are results of the country's turbulent past. The references to Nehru's Governments which made the princely zamidars give up parts of their state (11); reference to 1970, to Mukti Bahini (203); to the change of Government in Bengal in March 1968; to Mao and Lal Salam (293); to Indira and Rajiv and Sonia; to 1947; to the colonial past are all indicators. 'Sir' (Ajoy) a carry forward of that past. These events and dates are of continuity temporal time but timeless as the affect of these on tradition and the history of a nation is irrevocable. Similarly mention of old historical buildings and monuments like the Taj, Gateway of India, the Ghats of Benaras, the President's house in New Delhi, bridge the past and the present times. Calendar dating in chronological order is perhaps very easy and simple comparatively but in *Dying Traditions* dates and references to events are not just scattered throughout but are made to cohere. The times are not only revealed by the specific mention of a date but also as taking place at some certain time before or after some other event. For example Kripal and Vikram are friends in the USA but this is a consequence of an earlier incident in India in 1971. For an Indian reader in particular it is not difficult to comprehend and relate to the political and historical times mentioned in the novel as they are not far off in history. This by-gone period since it is not of a remote past needs no interpretation or explanation. In fact, by considering the past only half a century old Ashis Gupta is using the past for the purpose of social commentary.

Much different from historical times is the mythical time of the epics. Alan Trachtenberg in "The Journey Back: Myth and History in *Tender is The Night*" differentiating between myth and history writes:

> Myth tends to diminish the value of separate moments of experience by bringing them into a pre-existing pattern of coherence, while history tends to enhance the value of time as change.... Myth and history may stand against each other as ways of knowing the world, but both are relevant to the experience of literature.(135)

History has a one way flow. It is not cyclic. Historical time does not exist for mythical time. In the novel like the historical time mythical time is also contextualized. There is a mention that Sambhu Narain enacted scenes from *Ramayana* and *Mahabharat* (11), Dan is compared to demonology's one of the seven chief devils Mephistopheles (163); Alice is likened to Magdalena (179) the repentant sinner who washed the feet of Jesus with her tears; Alice refers to "remembering the voice in the garden. I was afraid because I was naked and I hid myself" (182); there is mention of Moses and the dove (290). These references by contrast or similarity bring out the difference between the profane and the profound, the sacrilegious and the sacrosanct, mortality and immortality, time and timelessness. Sambhu Narain like the timeless Shiv lives the life of an austere ascetic. He like Shiv is the destroyer of evil like Hargovind and the saviour of Krishna and Rahul. The three eyes of Shiv, one being in his forehead is an allusion to time – past present and future. Sambhu Narain also, connected with humanity, teaches men by his own example(a) the power to be obtained through penance (b) the great virtue of abstract meditation leading to spiritual knowledge and ultimately to union or actual identification with the great spirit of the universe.

Both Krishna and Sambhu Narain in the midst of life seriously talk of time as eternity. Referring to the Puranic division of time W.J. Wilkins in *Hindu Mythology* states that *Moksha* is,

> ...the dissolution of existing being... the absolute or final, Alyantika, is individual annihilation, Moksha, exemption forever from future existence.(355)

At Sanjit's funeral Sambhu Narain realizes that "till the beginning met the end and closed the circle, pain would return, horrors recur."(59) The novel ends on this note on time,

> Time which draws us out of darkness. Time which impales us in its hub. Generous Time which sets us free to wander on its rim. Cruel time which casts us adrift in the night as it spins along its endless course.(317)

It would perhaps not be too far fetched to say that in terms of 'yugas' – division of time as in the Hindu scriptures – it is 'Kalyuga' in *Dying Traditions*. It is the age of calamity, anger, distress, malice, cruelty, hunger, fear and decline in human values. Hamid's inhuman death, Saira, Alice, Chhotki and Krishna's mutilation of the body, atrocities during the partition substantiate this. Thus history and mythical times generate their own meaning.

In the novel, characters like Janki Devi combat time by lapsing into prayers. On her husband's death she "receded even deeper into the tomblike serenity of her prayer room... as if nothing had changed, as if it was just another glorious terrifying, day in her life...".(3) Sambhu Narain's asceticism is also a withdrawal from life and time. Krishna with her marriage, passes from one life to another. The six years of her married life are a normal period but with the mangling of her breasts there is a reversal in fond beliefs and a change in posture. To her then there is only the God of Destruction, and she "already seemed part of a kingdom out of bounds to most mortals" (299) In her insanity she transcends the pretentious needs and desires of this life. She, like her religious mother and ascetic father, is lifted out of the world governed by time and finally her suicide is the snapping off of time. Krishna's stillborn child, delivered by cutting her up, symbolically corresponds to the birth of Bangladesh. But it being stillborn is an indication of termination of life; suspension of time. Thus Sambhu Narain's renunciation, Krishna's insanity and her suicide, blind Malini and the stillborn child are disruptions in time.

These various time dimensions in the novel have been evoked with great success. The multiple point of views construct the narrative and the dislocation in time makes considerable intellectual demands. These complex ideas of time displacement are linked with a sensitive feeling in other areas. Sambhu Narain's recollections, Kripal's memories of the partition, happenings of 1971, Krishna's humiliation and in 1968 Rahul's activities and its effect on Rahul's life are also the historical and political past of the nation.

References

Eliot, T.S. *Four Quartets.* (1994) London: Faber and Faber Ltd., 1970.
— "Tradition and The Individual Talent". *English Critical Texts.* Ed.

D.J. Enright and Ernst De Chickera. London: OUP, 1962.

Gupta, Ashis. *Dying Tradition*. New Delhi: Spantech Publishers, 1992.

Marathe, Sudhakar. "The Beginning: An Exploration of The Processes of Initiation and Foreshadowing." *Narrative: Forms And Transformations*. Ed. Sudhakar Marathe and Meenakshi Mukerjee. Delhi: Chanakya Publishers, 1986.

Mendilow, A.A. *Time and the Novel*. London: Peter Nevill Ltd., 1952.

Miller, J. Hillis. "Three problems of Fictional Form: First Person Narration In *David Copperfield and Huckleberry Finn*." *Experience in the Novel*, ed. R.H. Pearce. Columbia University Press,1968.

Swinfen, Ann. *In Defence of Fantasy: A Study of the Genre in English and American Literature since 1945*. London: Routledge and Kegan Paul, 1984.

Trachtenberg, Alan. "The Journey Back: Myth and History in *Tender is The Night*." *Experience in The Novel*. ed. R.H. Pearce. Columbia University Press, 1968.

Trilling, Lionel. "The Sense of the Past." *Literary Criticism: A Reading* ed. B.B. Das and J.M. Mohanty. Oxford: O.U.P., 1993.

Wilkins, W.J. *Hindu Mythology* (1982). Calcutta: Rupa and Co., 1986.

16

Text/Subtext: Reading *A Fine Balance*

Ameena Kazi Ansari

Even though texts emerge out of a series of subtexts and they are artfully weighed against each other, Rohinton Mistry's second novel, *A Fine Balance* is an example of the superior kind. It is a saga that spans the momentous events of India's history from the turbulent times of the country's partition in 1947, through the horrors of the Emergency in 1975, to the macabre aftermath of its Prime Minister's assassination in 1984.

The story is built upon four characters whose predicaments intersect during the "State of Internal Emergency" declared by Prime Minister Indira Gandhi. Two tailors, Ishwar and Omprakash Darji, along with a student, Maneck Kohlah, are propelled by circumstances into the life of Dina Dalal, a Parsi widow, who struggles to make ends meet in a heartless metropolis, ostensibly Mumbai. Mistry manipulates the story in a way that the reader is shuffled between various time phases that mark each major historical upheaval. He highlights crucial events in the country's chronicle by depicting the background of each protagonist. The lives of the tailors' forefathers reflect the tyranny of the caste system in rural India where unimaginable horrors are perpetrated on the lower castes. In Maneck Kohlah's background lies the pathetic story of India's partition when religion became the unnatural reason for the birth of two nations. Dina's past underlines the sense of squalor and failure that middle classes often face rather helplessly in an underdeveloped nation struggling to improve its economic status. The combination of the real with the fictive gives *A Fine Balance* its peculiar flavour of the historical as the "contemporaneity of its texture and the historicity of its orientation together acts as a parallel for the lives of individuals" (K.Damodar Rao 128). The dominant setting of the novel is India's political milieu but to assess the novel in this perspective is to give it a restrictive reading. The novel is not a political one. It may be read as an effort at interweaving national history with the personal lives of the protagonists in a manner that is characteristic of immigrant Indian English writing.

The element of the humane runs through the novel which is "informed by the experience of double displacement" and is imbued with the authors sense of "identification with and alienation from their new and old homelands"(Bharucha 57). As a Parsi and then an immigrant in Canada, Mistry sees himself as a symbol of double displacement. This sense of displacement is a recurrent reality in the lives of the novel's protagonists. Ishwar and Omprakash traditionally belonged to the low caste of cobblers or "chamars". Social repression and bleak prospects made their forefathers push them into a more respectable profession – tailoring. It highlights the human will to disengage from the fetters of subaltern existence. In the novel, these men, though employed as tailors, are constantly aware of their roots within the Indian social framework and are beset always by a sense of fatalism and guilt that is the lot of the lower castes. As history would bear testimony, dwindling avenues of work economic compulsions and the lure of the metropolis take them away, like many others, from their familiar rural environment. They are two of the thousands of such displaced, hesitant, struggling individuals who fight incessantly to secure a a place in the maddening crowd of urban life. The emotional displacement of adopting a new professional identity and the physical displacement of moving to the city combine to give Om and Ishwar a yearning to repossess the simple pleasures of rural life. Such feelings are accompanied by a complex sense of alienation to which they finally succumb and end up as beggars on the streets of the metropolis.

Maneck Kohlah, the young man from the pristine slopes of the Himalayas, is another victim of this sense of double displacement. Apart from the geographical transition from the hitherto cocooned, secure recesses of the parental home, Maneck has to face the disturbing emotional displacement into urban college life. In an India trying to reconcile itself to the Emergency, Maneck has to swallow the insults of seniors and has to endeavour to adapt himself to the repressive political atmosphere in college. Mistry creates the character of Avinash, a fiery student activist, as a foil to Maneck and in the brutal political murder of Avinash, Maneck understands his own limitations and escapist tendencies. Unable to confront these realities, Maneck seeks a way out in suicide. This brings into focus yet another perspective on the sense of displacement in the novel.

For Dina life is a series of emotional upheavals and relocations of emotional anchors. Traversing the road of life, she is a lonely figure who experiences shocking forms of abuse. Her acute sense of displacement is more emotional than physical as her consciousness flits between ephemeral periods of happiness and seemingly endless bouts of pain. This may be marked in the dichotomy between her brief marriage to Rustom Dalal, her fleeting affair with Fredoon, her successful but shortlived tailoring enterprise and the abuse at the hands of her brother, physical intimidation by her landlord, the collapse of her tailoring venture with Ishwar and Omprakash, and her final humiliating return to her brother's house as an unpaid domestic. Dina's transition through life is cyclic in a sense. She begins life in her brother's house and after experiencing the vagaries of life, returns to it in a pathetic state of self-defeat.

It would be interesting to note the shades of J. Alfred Prufrock's sordid monotony in Mistry's characters. Their brief victories in life's long-drawn struggle give an overwhelmingly humane touch to the novel. Prufrock's sense of alienation, however, is not akin to Mistry's characters. Their efforts against the buffets of fate unite them and their glory lies in struggle, not victory. This places the novel many notches above a piece of pure historical fiction, or one of the picaresque tradition.

By "privileging the marginal" (Bharucha 59) the author follows the trail of post-colonial writing which negates the Western post-modernist stance that does not acknowledge the existence of a world outside the text. Situationally, it is the world outside the text that gives the novel its character and contributes to the impact of the plot. Rushdie sums up this peculiar propensity of immigrant writers in "Imaginary Homelands" when he describes their writing as an "endeavour to repossess their own history...whose fragments have been lost" (10-11). In a fictive technique reminiscent of M.H. Abram's lamp/mirror hypothesis, Mistry's writing becomes at once the reflection of outside reality and the expression of inner experience. The protagonists are the perennial victims, doomed to bear the burden of their country's chequered history personally and socially. It is these same protagonists who introduce a strange facet of incongruence into the text. Coming as they do from disparate social strata, their interaction would appear unreal to those who have had a close brush with realities of the Indian social scenario. It is impossible for such a reader to imagine, let alone accept, the close communion that Ishwar, Omprakash, Maneck and Dina enjoy. The apartheid of the strict caste system disallows such a communion and it is perhaps impossible for people of such varied social backgrounds to ever interconnect in such such close proximity with each other. It is here that language becomes the link and deregionalises the characters.

The writer is able to interconnect, on the human level, a plausible dialogue between the protagonists who hail from different linguistic regions that are a hallmark of the country's cultural pluralism. English, therefore, becomes a compatible vehicle for all the fictive characters to communicate in. It serves as the unifying quotient in the novel's realm of plurality. Mistry consistently uses Indian English, reinforcing, in the process, the status of the language as an Indian one with its own special syntactic and phonetic characteristics. In fact, he goes so far as to find it uneccessary to introduce any glossary to elucidate words like "*faroksy*" and "*kanasori*" which non-Gujarati readers would find difficult to comprehend. Language and characterisation go a long way in emphasising the "ethnic pluralism" Griffiths, Ashcroft and Tiffin 215) of Indian life and are reflective of the multiculturality of the nation in the text. In *A Fine Balance* language becomes a "neutral vehicle for communication between contesting language groups" (*Ibid.* 284) as Mistry succeeds in adapting a colonial tongue to local needs. This adaptation is characteristic of the postcolonial enterprise in which the essence is conveyed in a "language that is not one's own but a spirit that is one's own" (Raja Rao 296). This is the book's "international dimension" where in the writer's "national consciousness", rather than his "nationalism", evokes a humanist vision and negotiates between the meanings of cultural and political enormity (Fanon 199). Such a vision simultaneously strengthens the historical sweep of the narrative and liberates it from the narrow confines of time and space associated with a traditional historical narrative.

Arising out of these dimensions of the novel are the forces of conscience and conciousness. While the former finds its manifestations in the thought processes and actions of the fictive characters, the latter is implied in the socio-political leanings of the author in a social scenario devoid of all perceptions and practices of ethics and morality. Dina, Maneck, Ishwar, Omprakash and, to a lesser extent, Avinash and his sisters, emerge as conscience keepers within their restricted existence. By imbuing them with propensities that are humane, Mistry contrasts them with the savage allegorical figures who ruled the roost in the days of the Emergency in India.

In an inventive manner of characterisation, the author creates the persona of the administrator, the Facilitator, the Motivator, the Slum-lord, the Thakur and Bal Baba. Each of these men are parasites feeding on the helplessness and gullibility of the common man, destroying those who dare to question their ideology or defy their commands. The administrator represents the state machinery involved in brutal coercive sterilisations; the Facilitator and the Motivator represent the corrupt bureaucracy that takes a hefty cut for providing basic amenities; the Slum- lord and the Thakur are the agents of social repression, letting loose their goons on all those who try to break free from the chains of the strict codification of social groupings; Bal Baba symbolises the hold that ruthless godmen have over an illiterate, superstitious populace whose monetary donations pander to the desires of the godman's body rather than the spirit. History reasserts itself in macabre ways in this fictional framework. The story of Avinash has strong allegorical undertones as it has parallels with the tragic murder case of the engineering student, Rajan, during the Emergency. The suicide of Avinash's sisters is reminiscent of the combined suicide of three young girls in India's industrial city of Kanpur who could not bear to see their father's humiliation and social scorn for not being able to provide them respectable dowries for marriage.

Encounters between the symbols of conscience and the emblems of evil invariably end in the victory of the latter. The section entitled "The Circle of Reason" reiterates this dictum and leaves the reader shattered when Mistry sums up the dominant strains of the two protagonists destiny through the words of Vasantrao Valmik: "Loss is essential. Loss is part and parcel of that necessary calamity called life." This brutal truth embodies the writers consciousness which assesses the tragedy of history in subtle yet clear ideological terms. Mistry's perception of and reaction to the dark periods of Indian history are never clearly stated but are always implicity conveyed. The book stands as a scathing attack on the degeneration of political morals, agonising over the insensitivity of the ruling classes and coming down heavily on the subversion of institutions. Mistry makes no secret of his loathing for the powers that be and places the blame at the door of heartless politicians.

The central trope that unites the forces of conscience and consciousness is the image of the patchwork quilt. It is a piece of collective needlework that the protagonists indulge in after completing their respective chores. Made up of a number of left-over fabrics from Dina's tailoring concern, the patchwork quilt takes on the function of a *leitmotif* the novel. Each piece, different in colour and texture, comes to symbolise various memorable occasions in the characters' lives and stands for the alternating cycles of happiness and sorrow. Ishwar and Omprakash sum it up with the sensitivity of an artist surveying his world:

> Calling one piece sad is meaningless...it is connected to a happy piece-sleeping on the verandah. And the next square chapatis, then that violet tussar, when we made masala vada and started cooking together. And don't forget this georgette patch, where Beggarmaster saved us from the landlord's goondas....Before you can name that corner, our future must become past. Time is without length or breadth. The question is, what happened during its passing and what happened is, our lives have been joined together....Like these patches. (599-600)

The quilt takes on a number of metaphorical significances. On one hand, the lives of the minor fictive persona are reflected in its patches sown together; on the other, it highlights Dina's sense of despair and desolation at the end of the novel. This is evocatively conveyed when she perceives her life as a succession of images associated with specific pieces of the quilt. It becomes her "bed time story" as she returns to her past each night, covered by the quilt which remains incomplete as the last corner patch is never sown.

More importantly, it becomes a symbol of time as each piece constitutes the trials and tribulations or fleeting happiness that intervenes in her life and she adds a piece to mark the occasion. Omprakash sees time as a "bolt of cloth" from which he wanted to "cut out all the bad past, snip out the scary nights, stitch together the good parts and wear it like a coat, always live happily"(383).This intense yearning for happiness only serves to emphasise the sordid helplessness of each of the main figures.

India's pluralistic culture and languages, its extremes of rural and urban reality, parallels between the lives of individuals and the nation, multiplicity of voices and meanings, and the repudiation of the possibilities of absolute truth are all subsumed in the complex image of the *leitmotif*.

Ironic in vision, brooding in tone, amorphous in realities, *A Fine Balance* needs to be read as an expression of the predicament of self in the Indian urban/rural context. In spite of the stark life that it represents, the novel reveals an underlying moral purpose and a positive commitment to justice and humanitarian concerns. Mistry, as a diasporic writer, holds literary thought and literary language in a fine balance that is as much an act of "affiliation and establishment" as an act of "disavowal, displacement, exclusion and cultural contestation" (Bhabha 5).

References

Ashcroft, B., G. Griffiths and H. Tiffin. *The Post Colonial Studies Reader.* London: Routledge. 1995.

Bhabha, H. *Nation and Narration*. London: Routledge. 1990.

Bharucha, N. E. "When Old Tracks are Lost: Rohinton Mistry's Fiction as Diasporic Discourse." *The Journal of Commonwealth Literature*, Vol.XXX, 1995.

Fanon, F. *The Wretched of The Earth*. Harmondsworth: Penguin. 1967.

Kirpal, V. *The New Indian Novel in English*. New Delhi: Allied Publishers Limited. 1990.

Mistry, Rohinton. *A Fine Balance*, London: Faber and Faber. 1996.

Rao, K. Damodar. "Ordinariness of Dreams, Longevity of the Journey: Story, Statement and Allegory in Rohinton Mistry's *Such A Long Journey.*" *The Commonwealth Review*. Vol.5, No.1. 1994.

Rao, R. "Language and Spirit," in Ashcroft, Griffiths and Tiffin. 1963.

Rushdie, Salman. *Imaginary Homelands*. London: Granta. 1991.

17

A Literary Voyage to India: Rohinton Mistry's *A Fine Balance*

Savita Goel

The endeavour to write a novel about one's native country on the basis of memory has been an irresistible challenge and a compelling necessity for a number of exiled or immigrant writers who have been cut off from their ethnic roots. Their backward glance home conceals their desire for their lost home and their "criticism of the reality of home reaffirms the same longing, though in an inverted manner" (Kirpal 6). Salman Rushdie too, in *Imaginary Homelands*, contends that "writers in my position, exiles or emigrants or expatriates, are haunted by some sense of loss, some urge to reclaim, to look back, even at the risk of being mutated into pillars of salt" (10). The act of expatriation may result in the loss of "first hand knowledge of economic, political, social changes, of current jargon, of debate, even of such geographic elements as landscape, climate and even vegetation" (Parameśwaran 43), and it seems that the expatriate writer has to work harder than the 'native' writer to create authenticity. Any writer who writes about his homeland from the outside, must necessarily "deal in broken mirrors, some of whose fragments have been irretrievably lost" (Rushdie 11). Nonetheless, it is precisely the fragmentary nature of these memories the incomplete truths they contain, the partial, explanations they offer, that make them particularly evocative for the transplanted writer. For Rushdie, these "shards of memory acquired greater status, greater resonance, because they were remains, fragmentation made trivial things seem like symbols, and the mundane acquired numerous qualities" (12).

Canada-based, Indian (Parsi) writer, Rohinton Mistry's literary voyage continues to bring him to India. In his latest novel, *A Fine Balance* (winner of the prestigious Commonwealth Writers Prize, 1996), which is reminiscent of his earlier works – *Tales from Firozsha Baag* and *Such A Long Journey*, he again tries to revision the history of his homeland, his community and family and reveals his diasporic consciousness. The present paper explicates Mistry's nostalgic perspective of the political and social chaos underlying India's colonial and post-colonial experience. *A Fine Balance*, set in Indira Gandhi's India and more specifically during the time of emergency is a stark and moving portrait of life during this period. It reflects the reality of India – the predatory politics of corruption, tyranny, exploitation, violence and blood-shed. The paper also gives an insight into rural India, illustrates the injustice, the cruelty, and the horror of deprivation and portrays the trauma of India along communal, religious and linguistic lines.

While dealing with the lives of common people in post-independent India, the novel captures the socio-political-cultural turmoil of this period. Mistry achieves the remarkable feat of mixing historical slices with their personal lives and attempts to portray the reality of India by weaving together four worlds in the fabric of the novel. The first is the middle class, urban world of Dina Dalal, a pretty widow in her forties. Then there is a glimpse into rural India provided by Ishvar Darji and his nephew Omprakash – chamars who liberate themselves from caste stereotypes by becoming tailors in Bombay and gradually get caught in the quagmire of this nether world. There is another world symbolized by Maneck Kohlah, a sensitive Parsi boy, whose perambulations bring the reader occasionally into the predatory world of the university student. The novel is as much about the shared lives of these four major characters, who at one stage live under the same roof, as it is about their separate entities.

Mistry has concentrated on the pessimistic image of his lost motherland, gives an insight into rural India and mentions the atrocities committed on the untouchables. The chamars spent their life in obedient compliance with the traditions of the caste system and survived with humiliation and forbearance as their constant companions. Buddhu's wife refused to go to the field with the zamindar's son, so they shaved off her head and walked her naked through the square and Dukhi's wife was raped in the orchard. They were helpless victims and their crimes were varied and imaginative; a Bhungi had dared to let his unclean eyes meet Brahmin's eyes; a chamar had walked on the wrong side of the temple road and defiled it; another had strayed near a puja that was in progress and allowed his undeserving ears to overhear the sacred shlokas. When Dukhi became the father of two sons, he feared for his family's safety and as a precaution, he went out of the way to be obsequious. The children of the low castes were denied the right to education; Ishvar and Narayan were caned severely when they entered the classroom. When Narayan wanted to assert his right to vote, he and his companions were hung naked by their ankles from the branches of a banyan tree and the thakur's men,

> urinated on the three inverted faces. Semiconscious, the parched mouths were grateful for the moisture, licking the trickle with feeble urgency.... burning coals were held to the three men's genitals, then stuffed into their mouths. Their screams were heard through the village until their lips and tongues melted away. (146)

Their bodies were displayed in the village square and their entire family burnt alive. The writer, here, focuses on man's inhumanity to man and on the deprivation, inequities and injustice faced by the underprivileged in India.

The novel, on one hand, is a realistic portrayal of trains crossing the new border, carrying nothing but corpses, the conflict between the Hindus and the Muslims, fanatics burning shops and houses, involved in arson and bloodshed and the entire country in the grip of communalism. On the other hand, it faithfully describes the communal conflicts of 1984 caused by the death of Indira Gandhi when the Sikhs were ruthlessly burnt alive.

Mistry stresses the fact that in postcolonial India the plight of common people has not ameliorated and they have to face the same exploitation and injustice as in the rule of the colonizer, as one of the character says, "Of course, for ordinary people, nothing has changed" (581). It seems as if the native rulers have merely replaced the foreign rulers and Indian government has failed to resolve the basic problems of poverty, hunger, unemployment, illiteracy and disease. A considerable percentage of people live below poverty line leading a hand to mouth existence and the gap between the rich and the poor has widened. The writer draws a pathetic picture of near-naked people in Bombay slums, with meagre possessions, lean, emaciated babies, hungry and crying whom the parents fed with "half rotten bananas and oranges and scraps scavenged the night before" (330). The chill penury and wounds of India are shown too obviously.

> Outside the platform, a woman sat in the sun... drying her laundered sari, one half at a time. One end was wound wet round her waist and over her shrunken breasts, as far as it would go. The drying half was stretched along the railway fence.(281)

The writer, describes the saga of a poor old man who underwent a vasectomy, and his groin filled up with pus which lead to his death. He went in for this operation because of cash bonus and gifts, he had wanted to help with his grand daughter's dowry, again, portraying the shameful aspect of Indian society.

Mistry "finds Bombay oppressive and overcrowded" (Cyrus Mistry 11). When he went back to Canada he told Hancock that Bombay had appeared very grim and bleak to him, "Bleak was the picture I created when I was here. That's exactly the way it is" (148). The underprivileged section of Bombay do not even possess one square of land to live comfortably.

> Eight, nine or ten people in a small room. Sleeping one over the other on big shelves, from floor to ceiling, like third-class,railway berths. Or in cupboards, or in the bathroom. Surviving like goods in a ware house. (Mistry 471)

The writer presents a cross-section of Bombay – the huge slum across the road wearing its malodorous crown of cooking smoke and industrial effluvium, the long queue for water, accompanied by quarrels, lack of basic amenities, open air toilets, the familiar sights of beggars with their begging bowls and the beggar master paying the police every week to avoid harassment. Mistry's authentic portrayal of Bombay and its social ills such as child labour and beggary problem bears a close affinity to Meera Nair's film *Salaam Bombay*. The description of the beggarmaster with his imaginative mind, training his beggars and dressing them with a variety of wounds manages to raise a laugh as their chill penury is juxtaposed with the lighter side of their lives.

Depressed and demoralized by the ruthless murder of their entire family, pressured by joblessness and hunger and envisioning a bright future for themselves, Ishvar and Omprakash migrate to Bombay like Rajaram who says, "thousands and thousands are coming to the city because of bad times in their native place. I came for the same reason" (171) and "the city grabs you, sinks its claws into you and refuses to let go" (172). Their lives in Bombay symbolize the anguish, pain, anxiety and restlessness of people cut off from their native village. Like nomads, they moved from Nawaz's awning to their slum dwelling, then to the railway platform and then to the entrance of a chemist's shop where they were mistaken for beggars, compelled to slog as labourers and finally released form this inviolable hell by the beggarmaster. Their incapacity to find a home, despite numerous efforts is touching and pitiable. They are caught in an inescapable dilemma, between two worlds-their native village which they abandoned because it held a bleak chance and Bombay which has failed them despite promises-they stay on as marginal men, unable to discard the old and to find peace in the new.

Mistry discusses another perspective of Indian reality, i.e. gender discrimination and asserts that every aspect of Indian society is 'gendered' conferring specific advantages to men and disadvantages to women. Women are relegated to a sub-ordinate status in family and society. They are expected to be dutiful daughters, loving mothers, submissive daughters-in-law and faithful wives. Patriarchy defines the precincts of women and even a slight infringement on their part is sufficient to arouse the wrath of its representatives. After marriage women become the property of their husbands to be abused and bullied. Women are thrashed by their husbands, and if daughters are born, are ordered to discreetly get rid of the new born and they are strangled, poisoned or starved to death. When a son was born to Radha and Narayan, sweets were distributed and everyone rejoiced with them at the happy occasion. However, when daughters were born to them, no sweets were distributed. When Shankar's mother was born, her drunken father slashed off her nose in his rage, disappointed with the mother for producing a daughter instead of a son. Avinash's three sisters were aware of their father's sad plight at not being able to afford dowries for them. In order to spare their parents the shame of three unmarried daughters, they committed suicide by hanging from a ceiling fan. The writer highlights the injustices done to women, interrogates the marginalisation of women in the male-dominated society and contends that inequality between the sexes is caused by the cultural construction of gender differences.

Dina's brother, too, illtreats her, does not allow her to visit her friends, makes her do the household chores and she is expected even to polish his shoes. After Mrs. Shroff's death, despite her keen desire to pursue her education, she is not even allowed to matriculate. He tries to compel her to marry a person of his choice, but Dina protests and asserts her individuality. She marries Rustom Dalal, whom she loves intensely. Dina is the symbol of the 'new woman' who refuses to be acquiescent and submissive and does not accept the stereotypical, feminine role assigned to her. Even on that cruel night, when her husband died, she behaved in a very dignified manner, "No wailing, no beating the chest or tearing the hair like you might expect from a woman who had suffered such a shock, such a loss" (46). She refuses to disintegrate and resolves to restructure her life without being economically dependent on a man. Her quest for selfhood and her emergence as a strong, progressive and an independent woman forms the quintessence of the novel. She fetches two tailors, Ishvar and Om and starts working for Au Revoir Exports.

Through the world of Maneck and his friend Avinash, Mistry gives us a glimpse into the evils of Indian campus the shameful ragging, nepotism in staff hiring, bribery for admissions, sale of examination papers, special privileges for politicians' families, government interference in the syllabus, intimidation of faculty members and student politics in the campus. Avinash's death remains a mystery and the burns on the shameful parts of the body reveal that he did not fall off a fast train but it was the case of student politics and of wrongful death in police custody.

The Indian society is decaying from top downwards. The corrupt leaders have exchanged wisdom and good governance for cowardice and self-aggrandisement. For votes and power they play with human lives and accept money from businessmen needing favours. The pre- election speeches of leaders are crammed with false promises of powerful laws. For them "passing laws is like passing water, it all ends down the drain" (143). During elections, the illiterate villagers are cheated and the ballot papers are filled by men hired by the politicians. The novelist lays bare the election system of the world's largest democracy and the hypocrisy of the politicians.

A Fine Balance, reminiscent of Salman Rushdie's *Midnight's Children*, Nayantara Sahgal's *Rich Like Us* and Shashi Tharoor's *The Great Indian Novel* faithfully reflects the period of emergency in India, when the world's largest democracy spent twenty two months as the world's largest banana republic. Every atrocity known to have been committed during the emergency occurs to Mistry's characters and the novel becomes a template for a stark and unsparing portrait of that time in India. With the curtailing of the fundamental rights of the people, everything became topsy turvy, the press was censored, with the new law MISA anybody could be imprisoned without trial and there were countless deaths in police custody. Valmik, the proof-reader says, I am inspired by the poet Yeats. I find his words relevant during this shameful Emergency – "things fall apart; the centre cannot hold, mere anarchy is loosed upon the world" (556). Under the City Beautification scheme, hutment colonies were demolished and millions were rendered homeless, a new strategy was formulated for beggary problem and the pavement dwellers were made to slog like bonded labourers. The most brutal aspect of emergency was that anyone, young or old, married or unmarried was compelled to undergo family planning operation. Ration cards were issued only to those who had a family planning certificate and people had to choose between food and manhood. Incentives like transistors were offered for this, as in Salman Rushdie's story "The Free Radio". Ishvar and Om, too, became victims of emergency and the writer gives a heart-rending account of their vasectomization, the removal of Om's testicles just before his wedding and the amputation of Ishvar's legs, turning them into crippled beggars.

The novel is not just a sordid drama of their lives, it is also about caring and sharing and the close relationship that the four characters gradually built up. Dina's kindly gestures of applying balm on Om's hand, permitting the tailors to sleep in her verandah after their traumatic experience, Maneck missing his college and helping Dina to complete the dresses, their idea of eating together and the friendly moments they spend together brightened their bleak lives. Maneck feels that if "there were a large enough refrigerator, he would be able to preserve the happy times in this flat, keep them from ever spoiling" (440).

Dina and the two tailors have to struggle a lot and they encounter the challenges of their lives very boldly. It seems that they have learnt to accept their fate and to make the best of it. As Vasantrao Valmik, the proofreader says that "the secret of survival is to embrace change and to adapt" (230), one should learn to use one's failures as the stepping stones to success and one has "to maintain a fine balance between hope and despair.... In the end, it's all a question of balance" (231). Though, Dina in the end, becomes dependent on her brother, yet has a satisfying relationship with Ishvar and Om. In the end, now nearly blind Dina sits with her two erstwhile tailors, now turned beggars, feeds them with massoor dal and chapatis, sharing memories of times past and the novel ends with the warmth, thrill and pleasure of sharing.

The book is rich in a Dickensian cast of minor characters and Mistry succeeds in drawing a veritable gallery of memorable characters – the proofreader Valmik driven from his profession by a virulent allergy to printing ink, to a new job of hiring crowds and shouting slogans in rallies and the rent collector who cannot help smiling even though "his life had become the plot of a bad Hindi Movie, minus the happy ending" (90) and who at one point gives up, "It's no use. I cannot do this job, I hate it...." Besides these, there is Rajaram, who driven by extreme hunger transforms from barber/hair-collector to Family Planning Motivator and then to a murderer, who kills two beggars for their lovely hair. Finally, he becomes the highly venerated Bal Baba in a saffron robe and superstitious Indian crowds wait in long queues for darshan of this so-called holy man, who predicts the future. He has no charges, but all donations are mostly welcome by the Bal Bala Foundation, any much amount" (601). This provides another facet of Indian reality.

In this novel, like his earlier works, the writer once again succeeds in recreating the Parsi ambience. The rich culture, customs and traditions of the marginalised Parsi community are foregrounded and scenes describing the Parsi death rites and funeral ceremonies give the reader a glimpse into the Parsi world view. Faces like priest Dustoor Framji, known as Dustoor Daab-Chaab for his propensity to squeeze young women who come his way, and Dina Dalal herself, with an innate kindness that sits on her form like her favourite blue dress are totally convincing.

Mistry wants the readers to read his account of the myriad lives that animate *A Fine Balance* as a faithful rendering of reality. The Balzac quote at the beginning of the book, "this tragedy is not a fiction. All is true" seems to imply this. However, his vision is marked by pessimism and despair.

References

Hancock, Geoff. "Interview with Rohinton Mistry", *The Canadian Fiction Magazine*. No.65, 1989.

Kirpal, Viney. *The Third World Novel of Expatriation*. New Delhi: Sterling Publishers, 1989.

Mistry, Cyrus. *Sunday* 27 Oct., 1991.

Mistry, Rohinton. *A Fine Balance*. New Delhi: Rupa and Co., 1996.

—. *Tales from Firozsha Baag*. London: Faber and Faber, 1987.

—. *Such a Long Journey*. Toronto: Mc Clelland and Steward Inc. 1991.

Parameswaran, Uma. "What Price Expatriation?" *The Commonwealth Writer Overseas: Themes of Exile and Expatriation*, ed. Alaistair Niven. Bruxelles: Libraire Marcel Didier, 1976.

Rushdie, Salman. *Imaginary Homelands*. London: Gramta Books, 1991.

—. "The Free Radio," *East West*. London: Vintage, 1995.

—. *Midnight's Children* (1980) New York: Avon Books, 1982.

Sahgal, Nayantara. *Rich Like Us* (1985). London: Scepter Edition, 1993.

18

Remythologizing as Expatriate Vision and Art: An Intertextual Reading of Uma Parameswaran's *Sita's Promise* and *Meera*

Jancy James

The expatriate sensibility reaches out towards its cultural and ethical moorings in two ways: 1. down the memory lane 2. through a revision/reappropriation of history, epics, legends and myths of the native land. More than the nostalgia that attends these inner sojourns, there is a passionate desire and existential need to relocate the philosophy and vision of the homeland in the midst of the alien host culture. According to William Sofran, "the retention of a collective memory, vision, or myth about the original homeland – its physical location, history etc." is one of the six features of Diasporas (85).

For the expatriate Hindu writer from India, its epics, legends and deities function both as resource and stimulants for clarifying to himself the ethos and culture that he left far behind. In fact the people and place that he parted with have changed in course of time, and when he writes about his homeland it is often an anachronistic, outdated picture that he-presents either in terms of overidealization or condemnation. Such a long journey through an alien land and culture, through time and space, in all physical and metaphysical terms, is bound to defeat the expatriate writer's efforts to represent a true picture of what he abandoned on the native shores and what it has evolved into in the present.

But the repertoire of our myths and legends is an '*akshaya-patra* (the legendary vessel of Draupadi, that never empties) all writers of all times, that facilitates a revisioning of our ethos and culture. The *Ramayana* and *Mahabharata* have been decisive forces in the formation of the Indian mind. In moments of dilemmas and crisis of dharma the characters and messages from the myths in these mammoth literary sources emerge in the expatriate Indian mind as mighty sources of reference and clarification. In some writers, this urge for reference and clarification assumes overt representations, bringing in characters and contents from the epic sources, though in most writers, such referentiality is heavily encoded, and hence needs deciphering and deconstruction.

This paper deals with the conscious reworking of two important texts of Indian literary repertoire – *Meera*'s story and the Sita-Rama story – by Uma Parameswaran in the form of two dance dramas – *Sita's Promise* and *Meera*. The reworking has been done on two levels, both reinforcing each other, on the plane of art as well as vision. Aristotle had made very clear distinction between the two genres: epic and drama. And Brecht made a theoretical manipulation of this distinction by promoting an epic theater that hybridised epic and drama. Uma Parameswaran's competence and aptitude in dance and drama have led to a dance drama that made insightful use of the Brechtian epic theater. The Narrator and the slide projections in the backdrop interspersed with the thematised recitals of Bharathanatyam dance indicate the author's deft combination of the anti-illusionistic theater with indigenous art forms effecting a subversive use of the generic features of the original, managing a revision in terms of art as well as vision. The distancing and critiquing such a subversive art formula facilitated, stood her in good stead to remythologize the components of the repertoire that she boldly opened up. *Sita's Promise* begins saluting Lakshmi with an invocation dance "Vara Veena", evoking association with the curtain raiser moments of Yakshagana, the indigenous art form of Karnataka. An intertextual reading of the plays *Meera* (1972) and *Sita's Promise*(1981) leads us to the discovery of the three areas of remythologizing in these works.

1. Time
2. The bonding of the human and the divine
3. The imaging of the epic trio Rama, Sita and Lakshmana

There is an interval of nine years between the staging/authoring of these two works. Yet there are some crucial elements that impart a mutually referential and illuminating value to these works.

Time for the expatriate writer is inherently hyphenated, the pre- emigre and the post-emigre period. His experience of time is further problematised by the decisive shift from one's native space to the alien. Consequently the "discourse of migrancy" tends to address a "new epistemological logic" that suit / represents the corresponding Diaspora. In both *Meera* and *Sita's Promise* the central characters belong to as well as address a time-scheme that transcends the transience and mutability of clock time. Their selves cut across the barriers of death and period propelled by an inner urge to visualize the Eternal and the Everlasting.

Meera reveals at the beginning – "I live in the ever-present Now" (2). She draws sustenance for this unending continuity of existence from Krishna who "dances" in her heart in joy and love. Limiting the enactment of Meera's past story – her life as the victim in the hands of King Rana, her husband's brother – to a prolonged single scene in the Brechtian mode of narrational presentation (without any dialogue and with only Meera's narration) the theme of the play is centralized in the repeated birth of Meera in the form the various devotees of Krishna as Devaki, as Yesoda and as Radha These '*Janmas*' (births) testify to the ultimate unity of all forms that constitute Vishnu simultaneously establishing the timelessness to which He belongs, though his incarnations are tied to apparently timed period frames. Meera's *bhakti* for Krishna is the enactment of the finite reaching out for infinite (7) who inhabits the Eternal and Everlasting, Meera portrays this reaching out and waiting as the same as the passion of Radha for Krishna, Devaki's pained yet glorious motherhood and Yesoda's mothering of her mischievous foster son with adoration and nirvrti. Uma Parameswaran's proficiency in Indian dance [she runs a dancing school in Winnipeg, and is the founder of PALI (Performing Arts and Literature of India)] enabled her to realize the power of the art system of Indian dance and visualize any number of situations texts -- in a series of *bhava* renderings within a few minutes in a single recital. This is our indigenous form of the modern Transformation Technique of the Open Theater. It is capable of comprising the unending cycle of time through the *mudras* of *thandavam*. Though physically cut off from the native milieu of this art form, Uma Parameswaran makes use of it to reach out towards a vision that transcends all physical limitations, needing no time or space of human reckoning, an accomplishment made possible by the expatriate writer's nostalgic sensibility and talent.

In *Sita's Promise*, the concept of time is further elaborated on the verbal level itself through direct conversation. The story of the play is specified as happening in the eleventh month of the tenth year of Rama's exile. There is a superficial, human reference to the passage of time in the dialogue between Rama and Sita. "Rama, the years have flown by too too soon" (12) As the play advances through the reference to the cyclic and seasonal migratory flights of the bird Arctic tern that "divides its time between the north and south poles" flying 'twice ten thousand miles every year' there is also an underlying sojourn through metaphysical time that the play takes us through, made possible by the Divine interference that lifts 'the veil of Maya' and "perpetually exists beyond Time" (15). This flight across time in the late phase of their exile is undertaken to satisfy the curiosity of Sita about time: "'What's time ?" This mysterious time that make a day seem a year when you are away, and a year a day when you are near ?' (15) But even Rama could not give her a verbal answer to this query. Yet he knows that the experience of Time has two levels of awareness, "the human and the divine". (7) For the Divine, " the past, the present and future all come together as the Eternal Present". Rama says, "if the veil of Maya is ever lifted from us, we shall see as God sees for we shall be in Eternity, in the Everlasting Now" (5). Rama agrees to take Sita to the home of the Arctic tern in the far north, where Dhruva the star of the Pole stands overhead. But this gift of love is also shown to be a symbolic trip through space and time visiting future as well in which Rama's own future incarnation, Krishna, will be born. Their visit to Brindavan and witnessing of Krishna Leela is indicative of the timelessness to which the Divine in Rama is entitled. But his human self has to wait till the mission of his present birth is accomplished. This realization comes to him as he visits Lake Agassiz where Adisesha, the supreme Essence greets him as his son: "Not yet eternity for you, Rama. It is now time to return to Dandakaranya and make that visit to Sage Agastya" (23).

The discourse on human divine dialectics is present in both *Meera* and *Sita's Promise. Meera* is able to sustain herself in unison with the Divine because she worships Krishna, having given up everything of the world. Her mind longed to merge with the divine when she was alive and her brother-in-law's treacherous cup of poison only facilitates, ironically, her total delinking with the mundane, and her entering into the Divine self eternally. She then inhabits the all time cycle of Krishna's life participating in the re-enactment of Krishna Leela.

It is in the recreation of the characters, Rama, Sita and Lakshmana that Uma Parameswaran's expatriate sensibility has effected a dynamic act of remythologisation. Sita in this play is delicate, tender, possessing a childlike curiosity about everything around her. Her naivette is viewed with disapproval by Rama who suspects her competence to be the Queen of Ayodhya. But Lakshmanan has understood her worth better. There is a greater understanding between the two. He defends her whenever Rama underrates her. *Valmiki Ramayana* does not have such an imaging of Lakshmana at the expense of Rama. Rama's profound views on man, nature and God, and Sita's innocent and direct response to life are presented in a contrastive manner. Both Lakshmana and Sita tease him for carrying the permanent air of gravity about him. Lakshmana goes to the extent of blaming him for giving over importance to duty and neglecting the call of love.

> RAMA: (patronizingly) Where love conflicts with duty, it must be made to give way, brother, for Duty must always, but always, come first. But you know it already, Lakshmana, you have done your duty, forsaking the pleasure of the palace for service in the forest.
>
> LAKSHMANA: (passionately) No Rama. It was not my sense of duty but my love for you. Love. My duty was to my mother and yours who of a sudden were left childless; my duty was to my father, who might have lived had I been there to comfort him; my duty was to my wife, whose youth I have abandoned to fade and wilt in solitude and barrenness. What can you know of the soul's anguish or the body's hungers, my noble brother, you whom God has blessed with His perpetual presence and your wife's ? (17)

This dialogue on the conflict between love and duty is the author's own creation. Here there is an attempt at critiquing the rigidity of the Indian ethos that placed "dharma" unappealingly (to the mundane) and sometimes painfully above the interest of the individual. This is also perhaps the Indian expatriate author's effort to provide a corrective to the Indian code of righteousness. The tragic finale of the Sita-Rama relationship is anticipated in the highlighting of Rama's rigidity of approach to duty, a view point that later led him to abandon Sita. Rama is also shown to be submitting to a wishful thinking of the author about Rama's change of attitude in this play. He softens down from his superior stance of strictness, and agrees to go on a pleasure trip with Sita and Lakshmana. He realizes the folly of the fastidious nature of his expectations about others. Lakshmana's words had a chastening effect upon him and he repents. "Oh, Sita, all he says true. I am ignorant and conceited.

The sages gave me so much knowledge but the little wisdom I have received, I have received from you and him" (17-18) He steps down from his intolerance of human passion. He realizes the worth of human affections and attachments. He identifies the quest for God in human love. "But when you think on it, may be love is essentially the same. We express it differently to different persons – for mother to child to friend to lover" (19) Lakshmana is relieved at this transformation in Rama. "Wonders will never cease. My stuffy, pedagogical preachy brother has at last understood man's essential divinity, that we are all God within" (19).

Uma Parameswaran has placed Rama in his weakness and strength anticipating his abandonment of Sita and his essential goodness that grieved over the same act. The imaging of Rama in the play cumulatively effects an apparently binary vision – his essential goodness as well as the hardness of his moral code that underestimates human love and aspirations. The Hindu devotee in Uma Parameswaran's personality labours hard at justifying the cruelty of Rama's act. The Divine Mission that his human self has been entrusted with, namely the execution of Dharma, "Dharmasthapana", which ultimately caters to the merging of the human in the divine is repeatedly mentioned in the play. The complexity of the meaning and mission of Rama's incarnation is also subjected to an over simplification, possibly, to be comprehensible to a foreign audience.

Sita's personality fills the play with lyrical loveliness. One cannot miss the hurts that her tender mind suffers from a strict though loving husband. She is all love, compassion, like Nature herself, in keeping with her birth from the womb of earth as Janaki.

Uma Parameswaran has made significant deviations from the deoriginal source of *Ramayana* in conceiving the character of Sita. Sita is here imbued with a personality that is an admixture of her various selves that emerge on different occasions in *Ramayana*. She is in this play, all that one can gather about her after reading the entire *Ramayana* as well as Bhavabhuti's *Ut-*

tara Ramayana. She is naive, loving, yet courageous enough to question, Rama's rigid views. Sita of this period as presented in *Valmiki Ramayana* is a submissive innocent wife unexposed to the complexities of human behaviour. The author's anxiety to reveal Sita in all her humility and courage to a foreign audience has worked behind the imaging which involves the fusion of the early images of Sita with those from *Uttara Ramacharita*.

The creative vision that conceived *Sita's Promise* is crucially related to the expatriate writer's attempt at reclaiming from his native culturescape, some roots that would clutch in the metaphysical barrenness that paradoxically confronted him out of the apparent luxuriance of a materialistic culture. The Indian expatriate author has not only quested into *Ramayana* but also carried from it a precious content the problematic of Sita's return to the earth at the overfetishisation of Dharma by Rama, and resituated it on the host land, validating not only this ethically loaded feminine counter desertion of the patriarchal code of Dharma of the mother culture but also legitimising the author's own placement in the host country. Thus the migration of the Indians to the Canadian shores has been posited as a necessary act in order to answer the problematic of one of the icons of Indian femininity.

Sita's visit to sage Agasthya (as instructed by Vishnu) is appropriated into the blessed presence of the earth's daughter on the barren cold lands of Northern Canada. The touch of her feet turns the snow-clad land into a bloom. Hence, First Nations Children greet her as the daughter of Manitou (a derivation from Manitoba?) She corrects them and expresses her desire to show them the beauty of Indian "forests, our lovers, our elephants and our many coloured birds, and our warm sunshine" (23). The native children do not want their goddess to go away from them because they have seen "how flowers grow wherever she walks" and they request her to "make us more flowers, more grass, more monkeys, more of everything you told us about" (23). They implore her to stay with them. But Sita had to return to her motherland. The following dialogue indicates the author's ingenuous appropriation of the epic that lends itself to a "Spatial displacement that involves the internalization and projection of India" on to "another geographical space". As Vijay Mishra aptly remarks, "where epic textuality requires a fixed point of a past that cannot be duplicated but only extensively rememorated (and not displaced) what we get in the Indian Diaspora is a whole series of displacement to the construction of new spaces as metaphors of India (78).

> SITA: For a short time I stood on holy ground. (embracing a child) I wish could give you the beauty of our forests, our rivers, our elements and our many coloured birds, and our warm sunshine.
>
> CHILD: That's okay. Sita. We love you for yourself.
>
> SITA: How I wish I could stay with you in this lovely land.
>
> CHILD: If you must go, promise you will come back to us.
>
> SITA: I promise that, children, I shall come again to this lovely land of lakes and blue skies and snow. I, through my people, shall surely come again and we shall build our temple and sing our songs with all the children of all the different peoples who make this their home. (23-24)

Sita's story has been a fertile source for writers with the feminist agenda as a metaphor/example for female resistance to patriarchal predications of dharma. They have deiconised the submissive and all suffering Sita into a courageous person whose withdrawal from the male value world is pictured as a counter construct to Rama's self-righteous artifact of Prajadharma. Meena Alexander, wrote about "pale Sita", "preclude to ruin" in her poem "Sita's Story." In Malayalam literature, Kumaran Asan, wrote about Sita as a violent questioner of Rama's moralistic complacency.

Uma Parameswaran did not choose to tear the halo of delicate femininity that the Indian classical literary tradition has woven around Sita. She gave it added protection and stability by deliberating its continued relevance across centuries and continents. This can be read as an objective correlative of the immigrant writer's response to the problematic of expatriation, a willful and wishful privileging of stability to certain intimate icons of the native culture in order to ward off the sweeping flux of the host culture in which she has placed herself.

The hero, Chander, of Uma Parameswaran's story, "The Door Shut Behind Me" was given a copy of *Ramayana* and *Bhagavat Gata* by his mother as he was leaving the airport to take his journey to Canada. This was probably a metaphor for the *Ramayana* Uma Parameswaran always carries in her heart and in the springs of her creativity. *Sita's Promise* and *Meera* indicate the nostalgic passion of an expatriate writer to represent the characters and message from the greatest resources of her native culture with the help of her talent and learning and to represent them to an alien audience, earning from them if possible, the same love and regard that she carried within her for the precious givens that lay beyond the door she shut behind her.

References

Mishra, Vijay. "New Lamps For Old: Diasporas Migrancy Border," *Interrogating Post-Colonialism: Theory, Text and Context* ed. Harish Trivedi and Meenakshi Mukherjee. Shimla: Indian Institute of Advanced Study, 1996.

Parameswaran, Uma. "Meera: a Dance Drama", *Saclit Drama*, Bangalore: IBH Prakashna. 1996.

—. "Sita's Promise", *Saclit Drama* ed by Uma Parameswaran, Bangalore: IBH Prakashana. 1996.

Safran, William. "Diasporas in Modern Societies: Myths of Homeland and Return", *Diaspora* II Spring, 1991.

19

The Fragile Self-Image of an Immigrant Writer: Interview With Ashis Gupta

Veena Singh

Ashis Gupta, novelist and publisher, visited India in 1996. It was during this period that he came to Jaipur to participate in a seminar on "Expatriate Writing : Theory and Practice", and the following interview was taken:

Born in India in 1940, he spent his youth in Patna where his father was a medical practitioner. For his Ph.D. thesis he worked on the moral dilemma in Spenser's *Faerie Queen*. In 1971 he joined the creative writing program at Boston University and finally emigrated to Canada in 1978. At present he is a professor in the Faculty of Management at the University of Calgary. He was, for a short while, war correspondent during the Bangladesh war. In addition to the two novels *Dying Traditions and The Toymaker from Wiesbaden,* he has also authored *Ecological Disasters and the Management Dilemma : the Case of Bhopal.*

Here are excerpts from the interview.

VS : *During the seminar there has been a lot of discussion on "outsider - insider" situation of the writer or an intellectual. Do you think that the immigrant can become an "insider" at some point of time to his adopted new country?*

AG: I think the "Insider - Outsider" concept is really a function of the slot in the new host society that you get into. If I were indentured labour sent to Canada to work in the apple orchard of British Columbia or to construct a railway track at the turn of the century I would probably never be an insider. On the other hand take a case of a distinguished professor - one professor of English that comes to my mind is somebody like Professor Balchandra Rajan. He was a great critic of the seventeenth century. He taught at a university. A person like him would never be an outsider. He was really an insider. One can analyse what makes him an insider. Is it that because he was a Professor of English, in an English speaking world in a very English university ? Does that make him an insider ? So I guess it is a question of slotting. In a new society it is very much a function whether you remain an insider or an outsider. Now going back to Rohinton Mistry. Mistry himself, to some extent went there as an outsider. He went there to study English in Toronto and for many years he was teaching English and certainly had not found much space. Michael Ondaatje's family on the other hand is an extremely wealthy family. Very interesting. They are one of the richest families of Srilanka, and his brother, who actually sponsored him, is one of the richest industrial bankers in Canada. Ondaatje even as a young boy mixed with the top levels of Montreal. Thanks to his brother. So if I had a high society, a family background to fall upon I would probably never be an outsider. I didn't want to bring this up but I think it is worth considering what makes an "outsider" an "insider" or what makes an "outsider" remain an "outsider".

You may consider it impertinent on my part but I can not help asking you where do you find yourself?

Well ! I spent ten years in America, after that I have now spent, on and off, something like eighteen years in Canada and I have never felt myself an outsider. That may be because I have tried to create my own space and I really don't care where that space lies — outside of somebody's sphere of influence or inside of somebody's sphere of influence. To some extent it is not a question that bothers or has even bothered me. You might say,

"Well you are a professor teaching in a university. So you are already an insider." That may account for the fact that I have never bothered but even when you start off teaching you never are sort of secure. There are always periods of insecurity until you probably get a tenure or get promoted or something like that.

There has also been a lot of talk about the fragile self-image. How do you portray your fragile self?

Well ! I think anything can be fragile. I think everyone's image to some extent is fragile. But the point is that you take something that is fragile and you protect it. When you are young and you are growing into the formative stages you protect it through your family, through the love of your family, members of your family, people who are close to you and if that is not there, then the damage to the self-image can be immense.

On the other hand as I said every self-image is fragile. When you go to a new environment through immigration, whether you are a writer or not, you are vulnerable because you have left the protective cocoon of your own community where there is a certain identity, mingling or co-mingling of identity. You go to a new society or a new community you don't have that co-mingling of identity suddenly you see that protective layer is gone. You are almost standing naked as it were and that's where you have to create your own protection. I think, I said before, I found a bit of protection in the fact that in Canada, I immediately was in the teaching profession. That in itself is a kind of cover is it not ? The profession that you belong to, that becomes a kind of cover and you know, even if no close friends or intimate friends, that there is something. The university if they didn't value what little you had to contribute would not be paying your salary at the end of the month. So certainly that becomes a kind of protection for the self-image. I was lucky I did not feel threatened by certain social pressures. What does sometime threaten self-image, and certainly in my case also, is the danger of being seduced by some of the, you know, gross materialism of the west especially in a country like Canada or the U.S. and that is the threat where I think one feels, at least I sometimes felt, most threatened. How to protect myself from this consumeristic society where you know you have to consume, you have to buy even if you don't, sort of, say it yourself but it is always there. That, I think certainly to me, I felt was a bigger threat to my own self-image and what I wanted to be and what certainly I have learnt in having lived in India. I didn't go to Canada to improve my India living, that thought never even crossed my mind but I did feel that if I succumb to that, that would be a threat to my self-image and that to me was more dangerous than people telling me, "I won't give you a job because of the colour of your skin." The other threat is a psychic threat. When I use the words "in a venus-fly-trap" it is because often you get into that, a beautiful image of society, where you have every thing, all the comforts of the world, where every thing works. It is very easy to go complacent and sort of get lost in that without realizing, without sighting, like the fly there in a big jungle.

Do you feel alienated or homeless in Canada?

I feel alienated as a writer. I haven't severed my links with India. As the connections grow weaker the longing grows stronger. Parents of other exodus, that I know, they are certainly more anxious or more worried that their children are becoming less and less Indian. They do not even sense the nostalgia. They don't speak the language any more. They are not interested in Indian classical music. They don't know the Indian legends. They know the western legends and so on and so forth. I think the chances are that there will be more and more people who will, in the west at last, lose touch with their roots. On the other hand there will be the odd person, after all nobody is homogeneous, who will say, "hey ! I think I am missing something". That is what art is. So you will always have people who will come back with a sense of longing for something that is irretrievably lost.

When you write do you have the reading public in mind ?

No ! I think I have a reader and perhaps any reader. Once I was attending a class by John Barth, who is a well known American novelist but not ever widely read because he is an experimental novelist and somewhat challenging. He told me that once he was walking along a beach and he saw somebody reading a hard cover issue of his book and he said, "I just wanted to go and hug him because here was some one who had bought my book in hard cover and not paper back". So I think every writer sort of has this longing for a big readership but not thinking in terms of royalty or money but because there is something you want to share. If what I am writing is important to me and that is why I think I want to talk about it but who do I talk to if I don't have an audience, then I might as well be talking to myself. If you have studied Kafka you'll realize that Kafka chose to write in English rather than German. It was because of the large audience that he perceived in that language. I think today we are very fortunate for whoever is writing in English has a ready-made vast audience.

Yes ! there may be some people who do not like Indo-Canadian books or Afro-Asian books or Afro-American books but by and large there is no writing or reader community that is as large as the English speaking community.

When you write do you consciously identify yourself with some theory or style in particular ? For instance the back flap of Dying Traditions says it is a postmodern text.

No! not at all. In fact, I think often if you have theory in mind you probably end up obstructing the writing rather than helping. Theory comes after the fact. That is why theorists come later, writers come before.

Let me now come to your novels. In Dying Traditions were you, as an outsider looking at the immigrant experience and the consequences of immigration?

May be I was looking through Rahul's eyes. Probably, that is one way, I said to myself, Rahul is much younger than I was when I came to America. Rahul of course was a revolutionary in India. I was not. I think you are right. I was looking at things through different characters. This is what a writer does. If I were writing about a woman I can really never see the world through a woman's eyes. I can only pretend to some extent.

Your first book Dying Traditions is about India. The second novel Toymaker moves away from India and the third, Requiem for the Last Indian, not Indian in the sense that I am an Indian, as you mentioned, is still moving away. Is this moving away from India conscious ?

No, not really. This may seem very unpoetical, unromantic, I seem to stumble upon subjects. You know, grab subjects that sort of hold my attention and sort of work them through. Some of the themes, themes of myth, reincarnation of the spirit, are very much a part of our own culture of our folk culture which is not part of the west and for me to be attracted to something that lies in the native Indian culture is but natural. May be there is something even if I do not move consciously. The reason that subject A attracts me and not subject B is mainly because of some kind of cultural affinity even though in that way perhaps I ignore five different subjects because they don't attract my cultural affinity and pick the sixth one that does. But I am not consciously trying to move away from something, it is almost as if, I am being drawn to something.

Contributors

Professor Gurbhagat Singh, Department of English, Panjabi University, Patiala.

Professor Uma Parameswaran, playwright and poet, teaches at the University of Winnipeg, Manitoba. Canada.

Professor Ashis Gupta, novelist and publisher and Professor of Management at Calgary, Canada.

Dr. P.A. Abraham, Department of English, M.S. University of Baroda, Vadodara.

Dr. David Stouck, Professor of English, Simon Fraser University, Canada.

Professor Shyam Asnani, Department of English, Himachal Pradesh University, Shimla.

Dr. B.R. Nagpal, teaches English at Deshbandhu College, Delhi.

Dr. Rajul Bhargava, Associate Professor, University of Rajasthan, Jaipur.

Professor Jasbir Jain, University of Rajasthan, presently K.K. Birla Fellow.

Dr. B.Chandrika, All Saints College, Thiruvananthanpuram.

Ms Sonal Baxi, Research Scholar, M.S. University of Baroda, Vadodara.

Professor Jameela Begum A, Director, Centre for Canadian Studies, University of Kerala, Thiruvananthanpuram.

Professor Anisur Rahman, Department of English, Jamia Millia Islamia, New Delhi.

Dr. Sudha Rao, Associate Professor, University of Rajasthan, Jaipur.

Dr. Veena Singh, Associate Professor, University of Rajasthan, Jaipur.

Dr. Ameena Kazi Ansari, Department of English, Jamia Millia Islamia, New Delhi.

Dr. Savita Goel, Department of English, Savitri Girls College, Ajmer.

Professor Jancy James, Institute of English, University of Kerala, Thiruvananthanpuram.